Women Civil Rights Leaders

Lucent Library of Black History

Anne Wallace Sharp

LUCENT BOOKS

A part of Gale, Cengage Learning

Detroit • New York • San Francisco • New Haven, Conn • Waterville, Maine • London

LIBRARY OF CONGRESS CATALOGING-IN-PUBLICATION DATA

Sharp, Anne Wallace.
  Women civil rights leaders / by Anne Wallace Sharp.
    p. cm. -- (Lucent Library of Black history)
  Includes bibliographical references and index.
  ISBN 978-1-4205-0880-2 (hardcover)
  1. Women civil rights workers--United States--History--20th century--Juvenile literature. 2. African American women civil rights workers--History--20th century--Juvenile literature. 3. Civil rights movements--United States--History--20th century--Juvenile literature. 4. Women civil rights workers--United States--Biography--Juvenile literature. 5. African American women civil rights workers--Biography--Juvenile literature. I. Title.
  E185.61.S526 2012
  323.092'2--dc23
  [B]
                                                        2012028337

Lucent Books
27500 Drake Rd.
Farmington Hills, MI 48331

ISBN-13: 978-1-4205-0880-2
ISBN-10: 1-4205-0880-6

Printed in the United States of America
1 2 3 4 5 6 7 16 15 14 13 12

Contents

Foreword

It has been more than 500 years since Africans were first brought to the New World in shackles, and over 140 years since slavery was formally abolished in the United States. Over 50 years have passed since the fallacy of "separate but equal" was obliterated in the American courts, and some 40 years since the watershed Civil Rights Act of 1964 guaranteed the rights and liberties of all Americans, especially those of color. Over time, these changes have become celebrated landmarks in American history. In the twenty-first century, African American men and women are politicians, judges, diplomats, professors, deans, doctors, artists, athletes, business owners, and home owners. For many, the scars of the past have melted away in the opportunities that have been found in contemporary society. Observers such as Peter N. Kirsanow, who sits on the U.S. Commission of Civil Rights, point to these accomplishments and conclude, "The growing black middle class may be viewed as proof that most of the civil rights battles have been won."

In spite of these legal victories, however, prejudice and inequality have persisted in American society. In 2003, African Americans comprised just 12 percent of the nation's population, yet accounted for 44 percent of its prison inmates and 24 percent of its poor. Racially motivated hate crimes continue to appear on the pages of major newspapers in many American cities. Furthermore, many African Americans still experience either overt or muted racism in their daily lives. A 1996 study undertaken by Professor Nancy Krieger of the Harvard School of Public Health, for example, found that 80 percent of the African American participants reported having experienced racial discrimination in one or more settings, including at work or school, applying for housing and medical care, from the police or in the courts, and on the street or in a public setting.

It is for these reasons that many believe the struggle for racial equality and justice is far from over. These episodes of discrimination threaten to shatter the illusion that America has completely overcome its racist past, causing many black Americans to become increasingly frustrated and confused. Scholar and writer Ellis Cose has described this splintered state in the following way: "I have done everything I was supposed to do. I have stayed out of trouble with the law, gone to the right schools, and worked myself nearly to death. What more do they want? Why in God's name won't they accept me as a full human being?" For Cose and others, the struggle for equality and justice has yet to be fully achieved.

In many subtle yet important ways the traumatic experiences of slavery and segregation continue to inform the way race is discussed and experienced in the twenty-first century. Indeed, it is possible that America will always grapple with the fallout from its distressing past. Ulric Haynes, dean of the Hofstra University School of Business, has said, "Perhaps race will always matter, given the historical circumstances under which we came to this country." But studying this past and understanding how it contributes to present-day dialogues about race and history in America is a critical component of contemporary education. To this end, the Lucent Library of Black History offers a thorough look at the experiences that have shaped the black community and the American people as a whole. Annotated bibliographies provide readers with ideas for further research, while fully documented primary and secondary source quotations enhance the text. Each book in the series explores a different episode of black history; together they provide students with a wealth of information as well as launching points for further study and discussion.

Introduction

Unsung Heroines

African American women have always placed great importance on helping others within their community. They have long formed the backbones of their families, church congregations, and communities. Black women have also played significant roles in the fight for racial equality. In fact, the civil rights movement, according to historian Lynne Olson, "was a struggle that women helped to mold, lead, and organize from its very beginning."[1]

Starting with the abolitionist movement to end slavery in the nineteenth century, black women have championed many efforts to end racial injustice. They have worked to end lynching, have fought for fair housing, and have protested discrimination and prejudice wherever they found it. Black women, in fact, participated at every level of the civil rights movement. Those who assumed leadership roles, however, were often overlooked and given little credit for their efforts. Journalist Karen Jackson-Weaver elaborates: "Black women's invisible leadership has not only existed since the beginning of time, it was very present and pertinent in the Civil Rights Movement. . . . Though many times relegated to positions of obscurity . . . women were still able to make substantial contributions to the full quest for . . . freedom."[2]

Hundreds of women in the civil rights movement were not well known, either then or now. The majority were volunteers, such as the hundreds of church women who prepared meals, cleaned up after meetings, and marched silently and anonymously. These women went door-to-door working for voter registration, housed and fed white activists, and passed out leaflets and other information. Unita Blackwell, a former sharecropper and one of Mississippi's most effective organizers, once said: "Who's the people that really keeps things going on? It's women. . . . So in the black community the movement quite naturally emerged out of all the women."[3]

Well known are the names of such figures as Rosa Parks, whose refusal to move from her seat on a city bus sparked a boycott that was successful in integrating buses in Montgomery, Alabama. Also well known is the name of Coretta Scott King, the wife of slain civil rights leader Martin Luther King Jr. She walked side by side with her husband during the tumultuous years of the 1950s and 1960s and continued his work following his death.

There are other names, too; names of black—and white— women who made significant contributions and were leaders in their various efforts. Hundreds of these women played small but significant roles in the fight for equality. Joanne Christian, for instance, was a fourteen-year-old who combed the streets of Albany, Georgia, persuading blacks to register to vote. For her efforts, she was arrested thirteen times. Clara Luper was an Oklahoma civil rights activist who led a sit-in at a drugstore lunch counter in Oklahoma City; her actions led to the integration of lunch counters in Oklahoma, Missouri, Kansas, and Iowa.

Leading Ladies

Some women played even larger roles. In the late nineteenth and early twentieth centuries, Ida B. Wells crusaded in her journalistic writings and speeches for an end to lynching. Risking her own life, Wells spoke out against the horrors of lynching, the murder, usually by hanging, performed by mobs of people. Untold thousands of blacks, most of them innocent of any crime, were lynched during this period of time by white mobs.

Dorothy Height's work and leadership in civil rights spanned eight decades. Through her work with the Young Women's Christian Association (YWCA) and the National Council of Negro Women (NCNW), Height fought for equality and justice for blacks. Founding and participating in the NCNW's Wednesdays in Mississippi, she played a coordinating role between local women in Mississippi and civil rights workers during Freedom Summer. Freedom Summer occurred in the summer of 1964 and involved the influx of thousands of students to help with voter registration. Height also founded the Black Family Reunion, a series of nationwide gatherings that celebrated the black family and black culture.

During the Montgomery, Alabama, bus boycott of 1955, the name of Rosa Parks became well known. Another woman, Jo Ann Robinson, however, received little attention, but historians now credit Robinson with devising the plans of the actual boycott. In protesting the discriminatory practices on city buses that required blacks to sit in the back rows or stand, the boycott involved nearly all the black citizens of Montgomery. After more than a year, the U.S. Supreme Court ordered the desegregation of city buses in that southern city.

Daisy Bates, another civil rights leader, was the counselor and adviser to the nine black high school students who integrated all-white Central High School in Little Rock, Arkansas, in 1957. Throughout the ordeal, Bates stood by the students, acted as press liaison, and risked her life to achieve integration of the Little Rock school.

Ella Baker worked for several civil rights organizations; she is perhaps best known today as the spiritual leader of the Student Nonviolent Coordinating Committee (SNCC). Baker was instrumental in assuring this group was independent of the other, and older, civil rights organizations. She served as adviser to the group during the height of the civil rights era.

An Unequal Partnership

These women were often given little credit for their efforts. The media were focused primarily on such leaders as King, who along with other black ministers often marginalized women's efforts. Civil rights activist John Lewis comments: "There were very, very few women getting credit for their work, and even fewer emerging into leadership positions."[4] Nor was there ever a sense of equal partnership with the men of the civil rights movement. Historian Jacqueline A. Rouse elaborates: "Women in positions where they demonstrated important leadership skills often were

Civil rights marchers from Selma, Alabama, rest by the side of the road during the march to the capitol in 1965. Many women, both black and white, made significant contributions to the struggle for civil rights, though most are not well known.

not given the formal titles, nor the respect, their work deserved. . . . Women's activities did not fit the traditional definition of leadership."[5]

King and the other male leaders of the civil rights movement were viewed as leaders because of their position as heads of various civil rights organizations. They were often seen as figureheads who delegated the work to others. Women, on the other hand, usually led by example; they performed much of the work themselves. With the exception of Height, who was the president of the National Council of Negro Women, none of the major female figures in the civil rights movement served as important figureheads for specific groups. Instead, they worked behind the scenes, setting an example for others to follow.

Part of the reason that women often were not recognized as leaders was the mind-set prevalent during the early twentieth century and the actual civil rights era of the 1950s and 1960s. Although women had been advocating for equal rights since the late nineteenth century, very few gains had been made by the time of the civil rights movement. Men were expected to be the leaders, both at home and in the workplace. Women were expected to be their helpmates, not their equals.

Women clap and sing at the March on Washington in August 1963. Women formed the backbone of the civil rights movement despite being ignored by the media, which concentrated on male leaders like Martin Luther King Jr.

The Forgotten "Core of the Movement"

Female civil rights leaders were also often ignored by the historians who wrote books about the civil rights movement. The last two decades, however, have seen a reversal of the tendency to relegate women to a secondary role. In recent years there has been an influx of scholarship on such figures as Septima Clark, who helped educate the black masses about their rights and how to vote, and Fannie Lou Hamer, who was instrumental not only in organizing grassroots protests in Mississippi but who also helped found a political party. Clark, though her work with the Highlander Folk School, a controversial school that supported civil rights, and the Southern Christian Leadership Conference (SCLC), a civil rights group led by Martin Luther King Jr., spent most of her adult life working to improve the lives of her fellow African Americans through education. Hamer played her greatest role during Freedom Summer in 1964. Leading by example, Hamer's courage and determination brought thousands of black citizens into the civil rights movement. She was also instrumental in the creation of the Mississippi Freedom Democratic Party, a party that challenged the all-white Mississippi Democratic Party at the 1964 Democratic Convention.

These formerly unknown women played an essential part in the civil rights movement. Civil rights activist and former ambassador to the United Nations Andrew Young explains: "It was the . . . Fannie Lou Hamers . . . the Septima Clarks, and the uncommon black people of the South who, year after year, through their dedication and sacrifices made the southern civil rights movement possible. They were not the publicized leaders of the media . . . but they were the core of the movement."[6] Historian Garry Crystal agrees: "Women have often been forgotten about in the fight for civil rights. . . . However, women played a vital part in gaining equality and were an intrinsic part of the civil rights movement."[7] They were, in fact, the unsung heroines of the era.

Chapter One

Ida B. Wells and the Campaign Against Lynching

The struggle for racial equality has spanned multiple generations, originating before the Civil War and continuing today. This fight to end discrimination was and remains a struggle that black women have helped mold, organize, and lead. Ida B. Wells epitomizes the zeal with which many women fought discrimination and segregation. She represents the many women who followed in her footsteps by her willingness to die for what she believed and her determination to fight not just for herself but for black society. Journalist Jennifer McBride explains Wells's significance: "Ida B. Wells has been described as a crusader for justice, and as a defender of democracy. Wells was characterized as a militant and uncompromising leader for her efforts to abolish lynching and establish racial equality."[8]

Wells was never completely successful in her attempts to abolish lynching, the murder of often innocent individuals by mobs of people who take the law into their own hands, but through her journalistic and speaking efforts, she brought the horrendous nature of the crime into public awareness. Crusading in both the

United States and abroad, Wells risked her life to make Americans and others aware of the heinous nature of lynching and the reasons behind the crime.

Incident on a Train

Ida Bell Wells was born a slave in 1862 in Holly Springs, Mississippi. Following the death of her parents, Wells helped raise her brother and sister. In 1881 she and her two youngest sisters

Born a slave in 1862 in Mississippi, Ida B. Wells epitomizes the zeal and determination of many women who fought discrimination and segregation.

Sojourner Truth (1797–1883)

Like Ida B. Wells-Barnett, who would later speak out against lynching, Sojourner Truth was not afraid to tell the truth about another evil of racism: slavery.

Isabella Baumfree, also known as Belle, was one of twelve children in a family of slaves who were owned by several different plantation owners in the state of New York. When slavery was outlawed in that state in 1827, Baumfree's owner refused to free her. Rather than accept his decision, Belle took her youngest son and fled to New York City.

Years later, motivated by a religious vision, the forty-six-year-old Baumfree left her home in New York City and set forth across the country with twenty-five cents to her name. She changed her name to Sojourner Truth because she wanted to travel from place to place and tell everyone the truth about slavery. Standing six feet tall, Truth had a strong and powerful voice that often mesmerized her audiences. Despite being physically beaten for speaking out against slavery, Truth was relentless in her campaign. In 1850 she dictated her life story to a white friend. Another friend, abolitionist and journalist William Lloyd Garrison, arranged for the publication of the story, titled *The Narrative of Sojourner Truth*.

Following the end of the Civil War, Truth worked for the Freedmen's Bureau, helping the newly freed slaves get an education, find work, and locate housing. She dedicated the last decades of her life to opening the doors of freedom for all people, especially blacks and women. While much of her life is shrouded in myth, historians recognize Sojourner Truth as a nineteenth-century civil rights leader.

Isabella Baumfree changed her name to Sojourner Truth because she traveled across the country telling the truth about slavery.

moved to Memphis, Tennessee, to live with an aunt. While there, Wells passed a test that would allow her to become a city school teacher. When her aunt and younger sisters moved to California, Wells remained in Memphis, living in a series of boardinghouses and rented rooms while she attended college part-time at Fisk University in Nashville.

In 1883 Wells bought a first-class train ticket in Memphis, Tennessee, to the school where she taught classes in Woodstock, Tennessee. The conductor on the Chesapeake, Ohio, and South-western train asked her to leave the first-class car so that white passengers would not have to sit with a black person. She would have to move to the crowded and dirty smoking car, where passengers could smoke cigars and cigarettes; the smoking car also served as the "Negro" car.

Wells refused to leave her seat, pointing out that she had purchased a first-class ticket. She was then forcibly removed from the seat by several men; she fought back. Wells later wrote of the incident in her memoirs:

> He [the conductor] tried to drag me out of the seat, but the moment he caught hold of my arm, I fastened my teeth in the back of his hand. I had braced my feet against the back of the seat in front and was holding to the back. . . . He [the conductor] went forward and got the baggage man and another man to help him and, of course, they succeeded in dragging me out. They were encouraged to do this by the attitude of the white ladies and gentlemen of the car; some of them stood on the seats so they could get a good view and continued applauding the conductor for his brave stand.[9]

Wells was both furious and humiliated by these actions and left the train at the next stop. She hired an attorney to file a lawsuit based on an 1881 Tennessee law that mandated separate but equal accommodations on trains; she alleged that the smoking car was by no means an equal kind of accommodation. Wells sued the railroad and in May 1884 was awarded two hundred dollars in compensation by a Memphis judge. The railroad filed an appeal, and the earlier judgment was overturned in 1887 by the state supreme court. The judges argued that the accommodations provided for blacks were, in fact, equal in comfort and safety.

Career in Journalism

Following the Tennessee Supreme Court decision, a black church newspaper asked Wells to write an article about the incident on the train, the lawsuit, and the inequity of the law. In this article she emphasized that blacks needed to stand up for their rights, and her message was so well received that a number of other black newspapers and magazines asked her to write columns and articles for them. Wells was soon able to earn a respectable living through her writing.

Historian Karenna Gore Schiff elaborates: "For Wells, her writing . . . was her vehicle for leadership, her way to devote herself to the elevation of her people."[10] It was, in fact, through her writing that Wells demonstrated her leadership. In an era when few other writers were willing to publish such controversial material, Wells led by her determination to persevere.

There were several prevalent themes in her early writing. For example, she urged blacks to stand up for themselves and to help their own communities advance economically. She encouraged all blacks to speak out against discrimination and fight segregation in every way they could. She also urged blacks to become educated.

By 1888 Wells was contributing to black newspapers across the country. Often writing under the pen name "Iola," Wells met and networked with editors and journalists throughout the country. In 1889 she became a full partner in a local Memphis black newspaper, the *Free Speech and Headlight*. Her intention was to write for the thousands of ordinary citizens who wanted to be informed about current events. Wells explained: "I had an instinctive feeling that people who have little or no school training should have something coming into their homes weekly which dealt with their problems in a simple, helpful way . . . so I wrote in a plain, common-sense way on the things that concerned our people."[11]

In addition to her success with writing, Wells also continued to teach in the Memphis school system. In the late 1880s, however, she wrote an editorial in the paper criticizing the school system. During this time, black students were forced to go to school in dilapidated buildings without heat, water, or proper desks. They often sat on crude benches, used outdated textbooks, relied on teachers without the proper training, and walked miles to and from school. Wells called these conditions deplorable and shameful and charged the school board with being racist. The school system responded by not renewing Wells's teaching contract.

Outraged by Lynching

By the early 1890s Wells was a well-known member of the black community in Memphis. Two of her closest friends were Thomas Moss and his wife. Moss was among a group of blacks who opened the People's Grocery, a store intended to compete for black customers with a white-owned grocery store in the same

In the United States between 1880 and 1930 approximately thirty-two hundred blacks were reportedly lynched by white mobs.

neighborhood. Violence soon broke out between clerks at the two stores. Despite both sides being involved, only the black clerks were charged with the crime of inciting to riot.

Following the arrests, rumors quickly circulated through Memphis that black citizens were preparing to attack white businesses. The police were sent to arrest other blacks, resulting in the outbreak of further violence. There was shooting and vandalism in the black community, which lead to the arrest of many well-known blacks, among them Thomas Moss. While Moss and several other blacks were housed in the Memphis jail, a group of whites, led by law officers, entered the jail and seized three blacks, including Moss. All were taken out of the jail to a rural area and shot to death. While this was happening, other whites looted the People's Grocery and destroyed the store.

The murder of Moss and two other black men is an example of a lynching. The word *lynching* is most often used to denote death by hanging. It can, however, also mean death by any extralegal means. Lynching became a routine business in the late nineteenth and early twentieth century. "Between 1880 and 1930," reports journalist Clarissa Myrick-Harris, "approximately 3,220 black Americans were reported lynched."[12]

Despite the fact that the members of lynch mobs were usually well known to the police and the white community, few were ever arrested. The police, as well as local politicians in the South, condoned the crimes and occasionally participated in the murders as well. The white press praised the efforts of the men who committed these crimes, believing that they were ridding the community of threats. The press often used the protection of white women as the justification for lynching, claiming that the black men were guilty of raping white women.

In truth, Moss and other black businessmen had only threatened the profits of a white business. Throughout the South, whites were reacting violently to any evidence of black financial success. In fact, the South's economic and social system depended on keeping blacks in an inferior status. White Southerners were so afraid of blacks succeeding that many of them were willing to commit violent crimes such as murder.

Moss's death was eye-opening for Wells. When no one was punished or arrested for the murder of her friend, Wells was incensed. She realized that these whites were motivated by their fear of blacks achieving any kind of power, money, or status. Wells explained: "This is what opened my eyes to what lynching really was: an excuse to get rid of Negroes who were acquiring wealth and property."[13] She took immediate action. Following the murders, Wells embarked on a crusade to end lynching.

Antilynching Campaign

Wells's condemnation of lynching was fierce and angered whites in Memphis and throughout the South. She was also highly critical of prominent black leaders for their inaction. In an editorial, she called on black leaders in Memphis and the state of Tennessee to act: "Where are our leaders when the race is being burnt, shot, and hanged? . . . Our leaders make no demands on the country to protect us, nor come forward with any practical plan for changing the condition of affairs."[14]

In addition to writing articles, Wells also embarked on a thorough investigation of the practice of lynching. She traveled throughout the South, talking to family members and witnesses to the crimes, documenting more than seven hundred lynchings that had occurred in the 1890s. In the process she became the target of a lynch mob and was the recipient of numerous death threats.

Despite the danger, Wells warned the blacks of Memphis that one method of protesting the injustice was for them to leave the city and move west. In one editorial, she wrote: "There is . . . only one thing left to do: save our money and leave a town which will neither protect our lives or property, nor give us a fair trial in the courts, but takes us out and murders us in cold blood."[15] As a result of her editorials, thousands of black Memphians left the city, with most relocating in Oklahoma Territory.

In the eyes of the white South, however, Wells took things one step too far. In an editorial in the *Free Speech* newspaper, Wells refuted the myth that black men were raping white women. This excuse, she claimed, was often made by white Southerners to defend lynching. She used statistics gathered through careful research to prove that this was rarely the case. The white community in Memphis was furious that Wells had insulted white women in this way. While Wells was on the East Coast, a white

Harriet Tubman (1819–1913)

Like Ida B. Wells-Barnett, who faced danger and death for her stance against lynching, Harriet Tubman was not afraid to risk her life to end slavery.

Tubman was born into slavery. One of eleven children, she grew up on a plantation in Maryland. Following the death of her owner, Tubman heard that she and her family were to be sold to plantation owners in the Deep South, where slaves were treated even more brutally than where she worked. Determined to avoid this fate, Tubman chose to escape, moving at night through the countryside until finding her way to freedom in Pennsylvania.

She found work in Philadelphia and saved her money so she could return south for her family. She joined William Still, a black Philadelphia abolitionist, in creating a network of people dedicated to helping fugitive slaves. Between 1850 and 1860 Tubman made nineteen trips back to the South and led more than three hundred blacks, including her family, north to freedom. Utilizing the formidable Underground Railroad, a network of secret routes and safe houses, Tubman and others led thousands of slaves safely out of the South into the northern tier of states and Canada. Tubman never lost one person to the slave catchers, who offered huge rewards for her capture.

In addition to her work with the Underground Railroad, Tubman also served as a liaison between the U.S. Army and the newly freed slaves during the Civil War. She helped hundreds of former slaves attain self-sufficiency, nursed the wounded, and even served as a spy in a raid against Confederate troops.

Following the end of the war, Tubman made her home in Auburn, New York, and embarked on lecture tours to raise money for former slaves. She

eventually opened a charitable home for blacks in Auburn. Often referred to as a Moses figure, Tubman encouraged her followers: "If you are tired, keep going; if you are scared, keep going; if you are hungry, keep going; if you want to taste freedom, keep going."

Quoted in Catherine Clinton. "On the Road to Harriet Tubman." *American Heritage*, June–July 2004, p. 49.

Often called the "Moses of her people," Harriet Tubman made nineteen trips on the Underground Railroad to lead her family and three hundred other blacks north to freedom.

mob stormed her newspaper office and burned it to the ground. Her friends warned her not to return to Memphis; Wells never set foot in the city again.

Her Work Continues

The destruction of her newspaper did not deter Wells. Remaining in New York, she wrote for the *New York Age*, a black newspaper, and also for such publications as the *Indianapolis Sun* and *Detroit Plain Dealer*. She continued to write scathing articles condemning lynching. For instance, in 1898 Wells wrote in an article for the *Cleveland Gazette*:

> For nearly twenty years lynching crimes . . . have been committed and permitted by this Christian nation. Nowhere in the civilized world, save the United States of America, do men, possessing all civil and political power, go out in a band of 50 to 5,000 to hunt down, shoot, hang, or burn to death a single individual unarmed and absolutely powerless. . . . We refuse to believe that a country, so powerful to defend its citizens abroad, is unable to protect its citizens at home.[16]

In 1895 Wells published a comprehensive work on lynching titled *A Red Record: Tabulated Statistics and Alleged Causes of Lynching in the United States*. She argued that lynching was based on economic reasons and that southern whites feared competition from educated blacks. While perhaps one-third of lynchings were because of alleged rapes of white women, Wells found out that nearly two-thirds of all lynchings were based on petty incidents such as quarreling with neighbors or being disrespectful to whites.

Not receiving the support within the United States that she was looking for, Wells traveled to England, where she roused a great deal of antilynching sentiment. The Duke of Argyll, John Gorst, for example, was so impressed with her arguments that he founded the London Anti-Lynching Committee. Gorst and members of his committee later visited the United States, which further infuriated many white Southerners, who resented the English becoming involved in their business.

Wells's efforts, however, and those of others, eventually persuaded Congress to consider antilynching laws. A bill passed the House of Representatives in 1918 but failed in the Senate, due to powerful southern senators who voted against it. No law was ever passed by Congress to ban the crime. Despite Wells's failure to completely stop lynching, Myrick-Harris opines: "This fearless woman would do more than anyone to curtail the terrorizing of blacks by lynch mobs."[17] Myrick-Harris reports that due to Wells's campaign, the number of lynchings went down, "from a peak of 235 in 1892 to 107 by 1899."[18]

Life in Chicago

Wells eventually settled in Chicago, where she met lawyer and activist Ferdinand Barnett. Barnett hired her to write for his newspaper, the *Conservator*. The two were eventually married. Barnett would later serve as the assistant state attorney for Illinois.

In 1909 Wells-Barnett learned of a problem in Cairo, Illinois. Local sheriff Frank Davis had been accused of not providing his black prisoner with adequate protection. The black man had been seized from Davis's custody and shot more than five hundred times before being beheaded and burned by a lynch mob. Illinois law at that time stated that such law officers were to be fired. When Wells-Barnett learned that the sheriff was likely to be reinstated pending a court hearing, she traveled to Cairo. Convinced that any leniency would actually cause the number of lynchings to increase, she pleaded her viewpoints to the court. In part because of Wells-Barnett's testimony, Davis was not reinstated. Following her court appearance, many whites, appalled at the violence committed by the lynch mob, came forward to shake her hand.

Later the same year, on November 9, 1909, Wells-Barnett was present when a group of prominent activists, black and white, called for an organization to fight for civil rights. She was invited to the initial conference and gave a speech on lynching, asking the group to recommend federal antilynching laws. When a committee was drawn up to create the organization, the National Association for the Advancement of Colored People (NAACP), Wells-Barnett was not included. She was considered too radical a black voice.

THE NEW YORK TIMES, THURSDAY, NOVEMBER 23, 1922.

THE SHAME OF AMERICA

Do you know that the United States is the Only Land on Earth where human beings are BURNED AT THE STAKE?

In Four Years, 1918-1921, Twenty-Eight People Were Publicly BURNED BY AMERICAN MOBS

3436 People Lynched 1889 to 1922

For What Crimes Have Mobs Nullified Government and Inflicted the Death Penalty?

The Alleged Crimes	The Victims	Why Some Mob Victims Died:
Murder	1288	Not turning out of road for white boy in auto
Rape	571	Being a relative of a person who was lynched
Crimes against the Person	615	Jumping a labor contract
Crimes against Property	333	Being a member of the Non-Partisan League
Miscellaneous Crimes	453	"Talking back" to a white man
Absence of Crime	176	"Insulting" white man.
	3436	

Is Rape the "Cause" of Lynching?

Of 2,435 people murdered by mobs in our country, only 571, or less than 17 per cent., were even *accused* of the crime of rape.

83 WOMEN HAVE BEEN LYNCHED IN THE UNITED STATES

Do lynchers maintain that they were lynched for "the usual crime"?

AND THE LYNCHERS GO UNPUNISHED

THE REMEDY

The Dyer Anti-Lynching Bill Is Now Before the United States Senate

The Dyer Anti-Lynching Bill was passed on January 26, 1922, by a vote of 230 to 119 in the House of Representatives.

The Dyer Anti-Lynching Bill Provides:
That culpable State officers and mobbists shall be tried in Federal Courts on failure of State courts to act, and that a county in which a lynching occurs shall be fined $10,000, recoverable in a Federal Court.

The Principal Question Raised Against the Bill is upon the Ground of Constitutionality.

The Constitutionality of the Dyer Bill Has Been Affirmed by
The Judiciary Committee of the House of Representatives
The Judiciary Committee of the Senate
The United States Attorney General, legal adviser of Congress
Judge Guy D. Goff, of the Department of Justice

The Senate has been petitioned to pass the Dyer Bill by
29 Lawyers and Jurists, including two former Attorneys General of the United States
19 State Supreme Court Justices
24 State Governors
3 Archbishops, 85 bishops and prominent churchmen
39 Mayors of large cities, north and south.

The American Bar Association at its meeting in San Francisco, August 9, 1922, adopted a resolution asking for further legislation by Congress to punish and prevent lynching and mob violence.

Fifteen State Conventions of 1922 3 of them Democratic have inserted in their party platforms a demand for national action to stamp out lynchings.

The Dyer Anti-Lynching Bill is not intended to protect the guilty, but to assure to every person accused of crime trial by due process of law.

THE DYER ANTI-LYNCHING BILL IS NOW BEFORE THE SENATE
TELEGRAPH YOUR SENATORS TODAY YOU WANT IT ENACTED

If you want to help the organization which has brought to light the facts about lynching, the organization which is fighting for 100 per cent. Americanism, not for some of the people some of the time, but for all of the people, white or black, all of the time

Send your check to J. E. SPINGARN, Treasurer of the

NATIONAL ASSOCIATION FOR THE ADVANCEMENT OF COLORED PEOPLE
70 FIFTH AVENUE, NEW YORK CITY

THIS ADVERTISEMENT IS PAID FOR IN PART BY THE ANTI-LYNCHING CRUSADERS.

The National Association for the Advancement of Colored People (NAACP) was one of many organizations that publicized the horrors of lynching through the use of handbills such as this one.

Wells-Barnett was active in such organizations as the Negro Fellowship League and the National Black Women's Club, one of the first suffrage organizations for women. The Negro Fellowship League was a group that assisted poor black migrant workers in Chicago. Wells-Barnett was also instrumental in the formation of the National Association of Colored Women.

Mary Church Terrell (1863–1954)

The daughter of two former slaves, Mary Church Terrell dedicated her life to fighting for civil and women's rights. After graduating from Oberlin College in Ohio in 1884, she became a teacher at Wilberforce College, also in Ohio. She later married a judge, Robert Terrell, and moved to Washington, D.C., where she was appointed to the city's board of education, the first black woman in the United States to hold such a position.

After a friend of hers in Memphis, Tennessee, was killed by a lynch mob in 1892 in the same incident that caused Ida B. Wells-Barnett to take action, she demanded a meeting with President Benjamin Harrison. The president agreed to meet with Terrell and leading black advocate Frederick Douglass. After hearing their impassioned plea for a law to curtail lynching, the president, however, took no action. It was this inaction that caused Terrell to dedicate the remainder of her life to fighting racism.

In 1896 she joined other African American women in forming the National Association of Colored Women, an organization dedicated to improving the lives of black women. She traveled throughout the South, speaking about the achievements of African American women, and wrote numerous articles highlighting civil rights issues. In 1940 she wrote and published her autobiography, *A Colored Woman in a White World*, describing the prejudice and discrimination she had encountered throughout her life. She wrote: "As a colored woman, I may walk from the Capitol to the White House, ravenously hungry and abundantly supplied with money . . . without finding a single restaurant in which I would be permitted to take a morsel of food."

Terrell, at the age of eighty-six, later headed the coordinating committee for the Enforcement of the District of Columbia Anti-Discrimination Law. She presided over meetings, spoke at rallies, and led a group of blacks in protest at Thompson's Cafeteria in Washington, D.C. When she and her fellow activists were asked to leave the segregated restaurant, she and the committee filed a lawsuit. While the case was being decided, Terrell led the picket line day after day in front of the cafeteria. On June 8, 1953, the Supreme Court ordered the end of racial segregation in the District of Columbia. Until her death in 1954, Terrell continued to fight against racism.

Quoted in Lynne Olson. *Freedom's Daughters: The Unsung Heroines of the Civil Rights Movement from 1830 to 1970*. New York: Simon and Schuster, 2001, p. 76.

Mary Church Terrell helped form the National Association of Colored Women and worked to end lynching and racial inequality.

In the last years of her life, she worked on her autobiography, although the book remained unfinished due to her death on March 25, 1931. Her autobiography, *Crusade for Justice*, was finally published in 1970.

During an era when lynch mobs were common and black deaths were numerous, Wells-Barnett was one of only a few voices willing to speak out against these atrocities. Undaunted by personal threats and the burning down of her newspaper office, she continued to advocate justice for African Africans and an end to the violence being committed against them. According to historian Schiff: "She left a remarkable legacy and an inspiring story of how one individual can consistently stand for what she believes in, face down powerful forces, and take actions that will resound throughout history."[19]

Wells-Barnett, in her fight to end lynching, paved the road for the many black female civil rights leaders who followed in her footsteps. Her willingness to die for her beliefs inspired hundreds of other activists, black and white, to take a stand on behalf of equality and justice. Wells-Barnett provided a powerful voice against the horrors of lynching; other women would take similar stances against disenfranchisement, or being denied the right to vote; discrimination; and segregation.

Chapter Two

Dorothy Height and the National Council of Negro Women

When Dorothy Height finally stepped down as president of the National Council of Negro Women (NCNW) in 1997, she was eighty-five years old and had spent a lifetime, nearly eight decades, fighting against segregation and racism. In a speech for the occasion, Height stated: "I hope not to work this hard all the rest of my life. But whether it is the Council, whether it is somewhere else, for the rest of my life, I will be working for equality, for justice, to eliminate racism, to build a better life for our families and our children."[20]

Dorothy Height, in fact, had done just that for most of her life. Episcopal bishop Thomas L. Hoyt, in presenting Height an award in 2004 on behalf of the National Council of Churches, praised Height for her years of activism. He summarized her importance to the civil rights movement: "She is a living legend in the movement for civil rights in this nation. She has dedicated herself to improving the quality of life for African American women and children. She is known internationally for her work for human rights for all. The world is truly a better place because of the work . . . of Dr. Dorothy Irene Height."[21]

Born in 1912, Dorothy Height became the president of the National Council of Negro Women and worked for nearly eight decades fighting segregation and racism.

Early Life

Born in Richmond, Virginia, on March 24, 1912, Dorothy Irene Height and her family moved to Rankin, Pennsylvania, when she was four years old. The Heights were part of a large influx of African Americans who moved north in the early twentieth century in search of jobs.

Height's father was a self-employed building contractor, and her mother was active in the Pennsylvania Federation of Colored Women's Clubs. Journalist Lea E. Williams elaborates about clubs of this kind: "Organizations like these began forming in the late 19th century to counter negative stereotypes, decry lynching and Jim Crow laws, combat the woeful neglect of black women's health and well-being, and support black women's suffrage."[22] In her autobiography, Height describes attending many of these meetings with her mother: "There I saw women working, organizing, teaching themselves. I heard a lot about uplifting the race."[23]

When Height was a high school student, she became a finalist in a speech contest; the winner would earn a college scholarship. Just prior to making her speech, which focused on world peace, she was prohibited from entering a large hotel because of her race. Infuriated, Height immediately changed the wording of her speech. As she addressed the audience, she compared her own incident of discrimination with the biblical story of Mary and Joseph being denied a place in the inn. Height won the contest and the college scholarship.

She applied to New York's Barnard College but was refused entry because it already had met its quota of blacks. She later wrote: "Although I had been accepted, they [Barnard admissions personnel] could not admit me. It took me awhile to realize that their decision was a racial matter."[24] She was accepted, however, at New York University, where she obtained her bachelor's and master's degrees, majoring in educational psychology.

Height's first job was as a social worker for the United Christian Youth Movement, investigating the problems of young people. In the mid-1930s she became an officer in the National Youth Council and fought discrimination wherever she found it. She later wrote: "Thanks to the national youth movement, I was actively engaged in helping to shape the agenda that set the goals for which I struggled for many years: laws to prevent lynching,

Mary McLeod Bethune (1875–1955)

With donations from benefactors, Mary McLeod Bethune of Maysville, South Carolina, was able to attend college. After attending Chicago's Moody Bible Institute, Bethune returned to the South to teach. In 1904 she moved to Daytona Beach, Florida, where blacks were barred from attending public schools. Bethune opened a small school there called the Daytona Normal and Industrial Institute for African American Girls. With little more than a shack and a few amenities, Bethune and her school succeeded and grew; it later merged with Cookman Institute for Men in 1923, becoming Bethune-Cookman College. Today Bethune-Cookman is one of the country's leading black universities.

Bethune's friendship with First Lady Eleanor Roosevelt, who was one of the school's benefactors, led to her most notable accomplishment. Bethune became the first black woman to head a federal agency. In 1936 President Franklin Roosevelt, listening to the advice of his wife, appointed Bethune to be the administrator of the Federal Council of Negro Affairs. This organization was better known as the "Black Cabinet" and served in an advisory position to the president on civil rights. Bethune became an inspiration to thousands of other blacks.

African American leader Dorothy Height summarized Bethune's accomplishments in this way: "Mrs. Bethune fought . . . tenaciously . . . for black education and freedom. . . . She marched, she picketed, she boycotted, she signed petitions, she made speeches. . . . Many people called her the 'first lady of the struggle' [for civil rights]."

Dorothy Height. *Open Wide the Freedom Gates*. New York: Public Affairs, 2003, pp. 84–86.

An aged Mary McLeod Bethune (center right) stands with students at Bethune-Cookman College in the 1950s.

the breakdown of segregation in the armed forces, free access to public accommodations, equal opportunity in education and employment . . . an end to bias and discrimination."[25]

Young Women's Christian Association

In 1937 Height accepted a position with the Harlem Young Women's Christian Association (YWCA) in New York. The YWCA began in England in 1855 and, over the years, became an organization of women working for social and economic change. Height

A young black woman talks to an employment counselor at the Harlem YWCA. Dorothy Height became the secretary for interracial education at the Harlem YWCA, where she worked for forty years.

became the residence director of the Emma Ransom House, which was one of the few places in Harlem where black girls could stay while they looked for jobs in the New York area. While working there she discovered the danger many of these women faced. Black women, wanting to find work, were often required to stand on street corners in Harlem; people who needed work done in their homes would stop and pick out an employee. Not everyone was honest, and many of the women ended up being raped or exploited. Height testified about the problem to the New York City Council, but the situation continued.

In 1939 Height moved to Washington, D.C., and worked for the Phyllis Wheatley YWCA. There she worked with young black women streaming to the nation's capital during World War II to find work. Most of these women were unable to find housing because the city was segregated and had very few living facilities for African Americans. Height documented the problem and presented her findings to the U.S. government. As a result of Height's and others' intervention, the Lucy Diggs Slowe Hall was created specifically for black women.

In 1944 Height returned to New York to become the secretary for interracial education at the YWCA. In this position she developed guidelines about how to organize and work with interracial groups. She attended the YWCA's national convention in Atlantic City, New Jersey, in 1946 and supported the creation of a document called the Interracial Charter. Among other things, the charter declared: "Wherever there is injustice on the basis of race, whether in the community, the nation, or the world, our protest must be clear and our labor for its removal vigorous and steady."[26]

Despite an outcry by southern delegates who walked out of the convention, the charter was approved, and the organization began to focus its efforts toward racial equality for the first time. The YWCA became one of the first national service organizations to bring blacks into leadership positions and to focus on civil rights issues.

Height remained active with the YWCA for forty years. In 1963 she set up a meeting of YWCA officials and civil rights leaders. As a result of this meeting, the YWCA decided to allocate funds to help in the fight for equal rights and racial justice. A couple years later, in 1965, the YWCA established the Office of Racial

Justice with Height as its director. She was in charge of leading a campaign to completely eliminate racial discrimination within the YWCA. In part because of Height's campaign, in 1967 the YWCA announced that Helen Wilkins Claytor had been elected president of the organization; Claytor was the national YWCA's first black president.

National Council of Negro Women

In 1957 Dorothy Height was elected president of the NCNW, a position she would hold for forty-one years, even while she continued her work with the YWCA. Most of her work for the NCNW was as a volunteer.

In 1960, for instance, Height became part of the philanthropic Taconic Foundation, a group committed to furthering civil and human rights. Height joined an illustrious group of men: Martin Luther King Jr. of the Southern Christian Leadership Conference (SCLC), Whitney Young of the National Urban League, James Farmer of the Congress of Racial Equality, and Roy Wilkins, leader of the National Association for the Advancement of Colored People (NAACP). The group formed the Council for United Civil Rights Leadership and focused on allocating funds for civil rights; Height was the only woman in the leadership group. The group raised and donated nearly $1 million to help advance the civil rights fight.

Height and the women of the NCNW also participated in the much-heralded March on Washington on August 28, 1963. The purpose of the march was to demonstrate on behalf of jobs and freedom. Two hundred and fifty thousand people from all over the country attended the event.

As the plans were drawn up for the event, several prominent women, including Height, approached civil rights activist Bayard Rustin, who was supervising many of the details of the march. The women met with Rustin to discuss women's participation. Height, in fact, suggested to Rustin that it would be appropriate for at least one woman to speak during the program. Rustin and the other leaders of the march, however, decided against having any female speakers. No women were included in the program, with the exception of gospel singer Mahalia Jackson, who sang.

Height and the women of the NCNW were frustrated that so many women leaders had been ignored. Height stated: "We could

Eleanor Roosevelt (1884–1962)

First Lady Eleanor Roosevelt was often much more outspoken about civil rights issues than her husband, President Franklin Roosevelt. As a member of the NAACP, she lobbied for the passage of an antilynching bill in 1937, an effort that failed to elicit the president's approval.

In 1939 Eleanor intervened on behalf of opera singer Marian Anderson. Anderson had been barred by the Daughters of the Revolution (DAR) from singing at Constitution Hall in Washington because she was black. The first lady publicly resigned from the organization and arranged for the singer to perform at the Lincoln Memorial in front of seventy-five thousand people.

Eleanor's interest in civil rights increased as she traveled across the country and saw the dire living conditions of African Americans. She developed friendships and close ties with a number of black leaders, among them Mary McLeod Bethune and Dorothy Height. The first lady continued speaking out about civil rights during World War II. Insisting on social reform and racial justice, she campaigned for an end to racial discrimination in the military. She was successful in persuading the president to issue directives that integrated military facilities and military buses.

After her husband's death in 1945, Eleanor continued to speak out on behalf of civil rights. During the 1961 Freedom Rides, for instance, she supported the movement in her newspaper columns and speeches. She was also heavily critical of both the John Kennedy and Lyndon Johnson administrations for their failure to follow through on promised civil rights legislation. Historian Lynne Olson summarizes: "For many blacks, Eleanor Roosevelt was a true heroine, whose willingness to stand virtually alone and speak out for racial justice and equality was a source of great encouragement."

Lynne Olson. *Freedom's Daughters: The Unsung Heroines of the Civil Rights Movement from 1830–1970*. New York: Simon and Schuster, 2001. p. 61.

Eleanor Roosevelt (left) accepts the Mary McLeod Bethune Human Rights Award from her friend Dorothy Height in 1960.

not get women's participation taken seriously. . . . What actually happened was so disappointing because actually women were an active part of the whole effort. Indeed women were the backbone of the movement."[27] Years later Height reiterated her feelings as she told interviewers: "We were not able to get a woman to speak.

Dorothy Height addresses the press as president of the National Council of Negro Women. The organization worked to educate black women on their rights as citizens.

We accepted that because we saw that the whole objective of freedom and equality and jobs and justice was great enough for us to say 'we'll deal with this at another moment' and we did."[28] In her autobiography Height wrote that the failure of the male leadership to allow women to speak helped lead to the acceleration of the women's movement.

Height and the NCNW also played an active role in a project sponsored by the Student Nonviolent Coordinating Committee (SNCC) in the state of Mississippi in 1964. This project involved hundreds of young people, black and white, spending the summer in Mississippi, where they would establish freedom schools and run voter registration drives. Height and the NCNW were asked to send different teams each week to talk with local women in Mississippi. The purpose of these trips was to help local women become more aware of their citizenship rights and become voters.

The project was called Wednesdays in Mississippi (WIM). It was sponsored by the NCNW, with help from the YWCA and other women's groups. The group's main goals were to establish lines of communication with local women and lend a hand where needed. In addition, elaborates Williams, their purpose was "to quell violence, ease tensions, and inspire tolerance in racially torn communities. Southern women of goodwill, both black and white, responded positively."[29]

Height was part of the first team that went into Mississippi in the late summer of 1964. While there, Height attended a meeting of Woman Power Unlimited, a group of local black women who were committed to using direct action, including protests and demonstrations, to achieve equality. Wherever the NCNW women went, they were impressed with the dedication of the local women and the young people who were working on voter registration. The WIM teams were asked to return in 1965.

In 1966 the Wednesdays in Mississippi program was renamed and became the NCNW's Workshops in Mississippi. The goal of the workshops was to fight poverty. Underlying most of the discussions with local women was the urgent need to provide decent housing for poor black families. The team developed a plan so that the poor could own low-cost homes rather than live as renters. The NCNW team presented a plan to the U.S. Department of Housing and Urban Development. With help from philanthropic foundations, houses were built under a program called Turnkey

National Council of Negro Women

The National Council of Negro Women (NCNW) has been active in civil rights since its founding in 1935 by African American leader Mary McLeod Bethune. Under Bethune's leadership, the group worked closely with the NAACP, lobbying for the passage of antilynching legislation. The organization also worked on passing laws that would end restrictions that prevented blacks from voting and obtaining fair housing. In the late 1940s and throughout the next several decades, the group fought for civil rights and for school desegregation. The council also provided leadership and guidance to make African American women's voices heard in every area of social and political life.

From its inception the organization has offered workshops, training sessions, conferences, and other services. In the 1960s and 1970s, the council also provided scholarships to many civil rights activists who had dropped out of college to participate in the civil rights movement. The NCNW achieved a first in 1974 when the Bethune Memorial Statue was erected in Washington, D.C.; this statue was the first monument built to honor an African American in the city.

The NCNW has also been successful in enabling black women to design and implement programs in their own communities. One of its accomplishments was the creation of the National Archives for Black Women's History. This archives is home to thousands of documents from countless women's organizations. Today the organization is committed to strengthening the black community by focusing on black history, traditions, and culture. It has a worldwide outreach to over 4 million women. Writer Judith Weisenfeld summarizes: "The National Council of Negro Women (NCNW) has been among the most influential African-American women's organizations of the twentieth century."

Judith Weisenfeld. "National Council of Negro Women." *Encyclopedia of African-American Culture and History*. January 1, 2006. www.encyclopedia.com/topic/National_Council_of_Negro_Women.aspx#1 -1G2:3444700915-full.

III. Black families were provided with homes; no down payment was required. The NCNW then organized a Homebuyers Association, which trained members to manage and maintain their homes through cooperation. Two hundred homes were built in Gulfport,

Mississippi. Six years later more than six thousands homes in over eighty locations had been built as part of the Homeownership Opportunities Program. This experimental public housing program provided the impetus for similar programs across the United States.

In 1966 NCNW and Height also started Project Womanpower. The goal of this project was to bring thousands of black women into volunteer community service. With support from the Ford Foundation, a philanthropic organization that funded many civil rights activities, the first training session was held in New York State with ninety female attendees. Once trained, these women returned to their communities and recruited and taught other women to help in the struggle for better housing, improved schooling, and better health care.

Black Family Reunion

One of Height's greatest accomplishments while serving as president of the NCNW was the creation of the Black Family Reunion. Height explains: "We wanted a celebration that could serve as a rallying point for government agencies, private and public-sector institutions, corporations, community-based organizations, and families . . . to work on solutions to problems affecting the African American community."[30] The reunions emphasized traditional values in the black community.

The first reunion was held in 1986 in Washington, D.C., as part of the NCNW's fiftieth anniversary. Games, food, and music were offered, along with exhibits about job training programs, black history, and a multitude of other things. Other reunions took place in Philadelphia, Pennsylvania; Atlanta, Georgia; and Los Angeles, California.

By 1992 over 10 million people had attended one of the reunions. With a focus on black history, hundreds of thousands of teenagers have learned of their rich heritage. Journalist Clarence Waldron elaborates: "Height reminded the nation of the resilience and power of the Black Family with her annual Black Family Reunion festivals held throughout the country. She once remarked: 'We have survived because of family.'"[31]

Legacy

Height finally retired from the presidency of the NCNW in 1997. When asked about the issue of equality and civil rights that faced the United States in the twenty-first century, she responded: "I'm always an optimist because I have an abiding faith. . . . I think justice is not an impossibility. I think we can achieve it. But I must say that I am disappointed that in so many ways, we have the law, but we don't have the enforcement. There are so many things that are undone."[32]

Upon Height's death on April 20, 2010, at the age of ninety-eight, former president Bill Clinton and his wife, Secretary of State Hillary Clinton, remarked: "We are deeply saddened to learn of the passing of Dr. Dorothy Height, an icon of America's long march toward equality. . . . Dr. Height helped galvanize a movement that changed our country forever. She never stopped fighting for what

President Barack Obama sums up Dorothy Height's legacy at her funeral in 2010 by saying, "What she cared about was the cause. The cause of justice, the cause of equality, the cause of opportunity, freedom's cause."

she knew was right."[33] Sixteen years earlier, in 1994, Height had received the Presidential Medal of Freedom from Clinton. She also served as an adviser to every president from Dwight Eisenhower to Barack Obama.

Obama, in speaking of Height's life, commented that she had never cared about getting credit and often worked behind the scenes while the movement's male leaders earned more attention and fame. "What she cared about," Obama stated, "was the cause. The cause of justice, the cause of equality, the cause of opportunity, freedom's cause."[34]

Just prior to her death, Height was asked about what she wanted her legacy to be. She responded: "I want to be remembered as one who tried."[35] Journalist Rosemarie Robotham concludes: "She not only tried, she prevailed."[36]

Chapter Three

Septima Clark and the Citizenship Schools

Septima Clark, an African American teacher, challenged segregation throughout her life. As the education director at the Highlander Folk School, a school dedicated in part to fighting discrimination, and later the Southern Christian Leadership Conference (SCLC), Clark established Citizenship Schools that helped prepare blacks to become full citizens of the United States. In teaching illiterate blacks to read and understand their constitutional rights, she enabled thousands of blacks to register to vote and take part in the political process. Historian Lynne Olson elaborates: "Septima Clark had a genius for convincing people that they themselves could be leaders, that they did not have to depend on others to show them the way."[37] Clark, according to writers at the University of South Carolina–Aiken, earned the title of "Queen Mother of the Civil Rights Movement."[38]

Teaching

Septima Poinsette Clark (1898–1987) was born in Charleston, South Carolina, the second of eight children. She attended Avery Normal Institute, a school founded after the Civil War by the American Missionary Association; it was the only school in Charleston that prepared blacks for college.

Though unable to afford any additional education, Clark, nonetheless, obtained a teaching certificate. Her first teaching job was on Johns Island, an island off the coast of South Carolina. The population on the island was primarily black; most of the residents were descended from slaves and worked on white plantations. Clark arrived there in 1916 and found the black schools very primitive; her students ranged in age from the very young to much older children. At one point she taught over 130 students for thirty-five dollars a month.

Clark was a natural teacher and loved working with young people. Since there were no textbooks of any kind, she talked to the students and had them share stories about the island and their homes. There was no chalkboard, so she wrote out these stories on old paper bags; she then used this material in teaching them to read and write. She also began teaching many of their parents, most of whom could neither read nor write. She also organized a parent-teacher group and gradually began to create textbooks and improve school conditions on the island.

After three years on Johns Island, Clark returned to Charleston to teach at Avery Normal. She also joined the National Association for the Advancement of Colored People (NAACP) and became active in that organization's efforts to force the state of South Carolina to hire black teachers in its public schools. Thanks to the efforts of the NAACP, the state passed a statute in 1920 that allowed black teachers to do so; a year later Clark was hired to teach elementary school in the city.

In the late 1920s she met and married a young navy cook named Nerie Clark. After Nerie's discharge from the service, the couple moved to Dayton, Ohio. When Septima found out her husband had a mistress, she left him and moved to Hickory, North Carolina, to live with his parents. Nerie died shortly thereafter. Following his death Septima moved to Columbia, South Carolina, where she taught in an elementary school. She also took summer classes at several universities and eventually earned both her bachelor's and master's degrees. She taught school in Columbia for eighteen years.

While in Columbia, Clark also began to work in the kind of citizenship education programs she would later lead. She was asked by Wil Lou Gray, head of the South Carolina Adult Education Program, to help educate illiterate African American sol-

Septima Clark's (seated) genius lay in convincing people that they themselves could become leaders and that they did not need others to show them the way. She is often called "the queen mother of the civil rights movement."

diers who were stationed at nearby Camp Jackson. This program trained soldiers to learn to sign their names to pay slips, read bus routes, and learn to count.

Highlander Folk School

In 1947 Clark moved back to Charleston to take care of her ailing mother. Active in Charleston's black community and well respected in the school system, Clark was always on the lookout for ways to increase her knowledge. In 1954 she decided to attend a workshop at Highlander Folk School at the suggestion of another teacher. The school, located in rural Tennessee, brought together people from all over the country to participate in integrated workshops. In these sessions people learned about community organizing, voter registration, and civil rights activism. Historian Jacqueline A. Rouse explains: "Advocating equality of the races, Highlander flagrantly violated segregation laws and customs, and provided integrated housing and other accommodations. Highlander sponsored workshops which concentrated on the elimination of racial stereotypes, the breaking down of social barriers, and the development of leaders."[39]

Clark was excited about what she had learned at Highlander. When she returned to Charleston, she began organizing black teachers, many of whom were having difficulty getting loans to attend graduate programs. White teachers, on the other hand, seldom had any problem qualifying for such loans. With Clark's guidance, the teachers remedied the situation by opening their own credit union.

It was around this time that the landmark decision of *Brown v. Board of Education of Topeka, Kansas* was handed down by the U.S. Supreme Court. On May 17, 1954, the court declared that school segregation was unconstitutional. White outrage about this decision led to numerous southern state governments announcing that they would not abide by the court ruling.

South Carolina passed a law that stated that no city or state employee could belong to the NAACP. Then the Charleston School Board, in an attempt to determine the loyalty of their employees, also began requiring that all their public school teachers list their organizational affiliations on a questionnaire. When Clark listed her membership in the NAACP, she was summarily fired from her teaching job and denied her pension. Almost sixty years old, and after forty years of teaching, Clark found that she was unemployed and without any money to support herself.

When the director of Highlander Folk School, Myles Horton, heard that Clark was out of work, he offered her the job of director of workshops at the school. He wanted Clark to focus on providing blacks with the necessary literacy skills to become registered voters. To accomplish this Clark developed what she referred to as the "Two-Eye" theory of education. She used one eye to gather students' views on what they needed to learn and the other eye to picture strategies and teaching methods that would help the students meet their needs.

Clark used people's own experiences to improve their reading and writing skills. Participants, for instance, learned to read the Bible, the newspaper, and road signs, while also learning to write their own names. Clark also spent large amounts of time preparing attendees on the best way to register to vote by coaching them on how to pass the literacy tests. She also wrote several workbooks such as *Taxes You Must Pay* to prepare students to become full citizens. Historian Taylor Branch summarizes: "In a compressed week's workshop, Clark promised to turn sharecroppers and other unschooled Negroes into potential voters, armed with basic literacy and a grasp of democratic rights."[40]

In the meantime, the Highlander Folk School came under increasing scrutiny from the white Tennessee government. State leaders were determined to shut down the school because of its integration policies and citizenship teachings; when legal reasons could not be found, state authorities resorted to other methods. One night in 1959, a group of policemen showed up and burst into the assembly hall. Led by Tennessee attorney general Ab Sloan, the men presented Clark with a warrant to search the premises for liquor. While they found no alcohol except in one small home on the school grounds, the police arrested Clark and three men and took them to jail in Altamont, Tennessee. While at the school, the police seized personal belongings and destroyed many Highlander documents. Clark was later released on bail.

On August 6, 1959, a preliminary hearing on the liquor charge was held. One state witness claimed that he had seen an interracial couple having sex in the school library. The problem with

Highlander Folk School

Highlander Folk School was founded in 1932 by educator Myles Horton. During its first two decades, the school focused on teaching workers in the Appalachian Mountains about such labor issues as organizing, protesting, and worker education.

In the 1950s, particularly after the landmark *Brown v. Board of Education* ruling in 1954 that ordered the desegregation of public schools, Highlander began to focus exclusively on civil rights issues. Horton and his teachers taught people from all across the country about civil disobedience, different forms of protest, and constitutional rights. Historian Herb Boyd elaborates: "At the core of Horton's mission was the belief that people could solve their own problems with proper guidance and leadership. They could be agents of their own liberation."

A large number of civil rights leaders attended the school during the 1950s and early 1960s, including Martin Luther King Jr. Its graduates also included Rosa Parks and Fannie Lou Hamer, two women who would play significant roles in the civil rights movement.

In rural Tennessee, however, such a school where integration was accepted and advocated was considered dangerous by white authorities. Beginning in the 1950s the state legislature began to look for ways to shut down the school and revoke its nonprofit charter. A committee was formed and began to hear testimony that the school was indulging in questionable activity. The state of Tennessee eventually revoked the charter of the school, and it closed in 1961.

The school relocated to Knoxville, Tennessee, in the 1980s and became the Highlander Research and Education Center. Today it focuses on economic justice and democratic participation.

Herb Boyd. *We Shall Overcome*. Naperville, IL: Sourcebooks, 2004, p. 48.

(Left to right) Martin Luther King Jr., Pete Seeger, Charis Horton, Rosa Parks, and Ralph Abernathy stand in front of the library at Highland Folk School.

this story was that the occurrence was alleged to have taken place before the library was even built. Others testified that liquor was routinely served at the school. The court eventually upheld the charges. On September 16, 1959, the judge ordered the administration building closed, and in February 1960 a Grundy County circuit court judge revoked the school's charter. The school lost its final appeal in April 1961 and closed its doors. It reopened in the 1980s with a focus on economic issues.

Citizenship Schools

While these trials were taking place, Horton got in contact with the SCLC about that organization taking over the citizenship classes. The SCLC was founded in 1957 and had almost immediately begun a Crusade for Citizenship program aimed at increasing the number of black voters.

The Crusade for Citizenship program was unsuccessful primarily because the majority of blacks could not pass a literacy test that was required by voter registrars. When Martin Luther King Jr. and the other leaders of the SCLC heard of Clark's success at Highlander, they decided to offer her a similar position with their organization. In 1961 Clark accepted King's invitation to serve as director of education and teaching for the SCLC.

Clark's most significant contribution to the SCLC became the Voter Education Project, which was devised to teach potential voters how to register. She stated: "I went to SCLC and worked with Dr. King as director of education and director of teaching. And there traveled from place to place getting people to realize that they wanted to eliminate illiteracy. We had to eliminate illiteracy first! And then after eliminating illiteracy, then we went into registration and voting."[41]

The citizenship program had its headquarters in Dorchester, Georgia. While Clark led the citizenship classes, King's protégé Andrew Young was in charge of the overall program. Young's main purpose was to make contact with northern philanthropists for funds to help finance voter education and eventual registration. The Citizenship Schools were funded by grants from the Ford Foundation and the Marshall Field Foundation, among others.

When the program participants came to Dorchester or other locations, they came in buses and arrived on Sunday nights. During

Voting Restrictions

White southern governments took a number of measures to keep African Americans from voting. Many southern states, for instance, required potential voters to take literacy tests; other states had expensive poll taxes; and nearly every southern state used intimidation and violence to keep blacks from voting. These same techniques were occasionally used elsewhere.

In most southern states people were required to take a literacy test before they could register to vote; the literacy test, however, was rarely administered to white voters. Southern writer George C. Stoney explains: "Electors are required to read, write, and explain any passage of the state constitution chosen by the registrar, who is the sole and final judge. Many Negro professors have been denied the ballot under such procedures." In several documented instances, blacks who correctly interpreted the constitution were then required to read other documents written in foreign languages. The tests were thus created so that blacks would fail them.

In addition to the literacy test, many southern states also used the poll tax to restrict black voter registration. Poll taxes, a tax that a person had to pay in order to vote, began in the late nineteenth century as an effort to keep blacks from voting; blacks could not afford to pay them. In addition to these measures, other tactics were used by registrars to keep blacks from voting. Intimidation was frequently used; white racist groups such as the Ku Klux Klan often patrolled areas in the South where blacks attempted to register. Violence was common as blacks who tried to vote were attacked and threatened.

Quoted in Karenna Gore Schiff. *Lighting the Way: Nine Women Who Changed Modern America.* New York: Hyperion, 2005, p. 289.

A man practices taking a "literacy test" in South Carolina in 1962. Literacy tests were intended to disqualify African American voters.

Church and civil rights leaders discuss voter education efforts. Septima Clark's Voter Education Project was a significant contribution to this cause.

the week, they attended classes that brought together people, black and white, from all over the South. Part of Clark's gift, according to Branch, was "recognizing natural leaders among the poorly educated yeomanry—midwives, old farmers . . . grandmothers . . . and imparting to them her unshakable confidence and respect."[42]

Clark and the other teachers taught by asking questions such as "What does it mean to be a U.S. citizen?" The teachers utilized such things as newspapers and street signs to teach literacy. The students also learned to fill out Social Security forms, money orders, catalog forms, tax returns, applications for driver's licenses, and job applications. In math classes the students were taught how much money was needed for gas or the length of fencing needed to encircle a field. There were also sessions on black history and classes on nonviolent protest.

Citizenship Schools were established in eleven different southern states. To make the classes effective in each region, Clark gathered information about local and state voting requirements, since each state had different laws. Clark explains: "We used the election laws of that particular state to teach the reading. Each state had to have its own particular reading, because each state had different requirements for the election laws."[43] Participants left the workshops with a determination to register to vote and to pass on the skills they had learned to others in their own communities. Branch summarizes how effective the study program was: "With drills from basic civics—how to spell 'freedom,' the basic duties of a sheriff—Clark needed only an intensive week's retreat to have most former illiterates proudly signing their names, writing letters, and lining up at the courthouse, able and inspired to register."[44]

For her job, Clark traveled throughout the South recruiting and teaching. Every teacher she trained came from the community in which that person later taught. Women predominated as both teachers and students in the Citizenship Schools. Journalists Katherine Mellen Charron and David P. Cline elaborate:

> Training sessions and teaching classes afforded grassroots African American women the opportunity to evaluate the local problems they deemed most important while the Movement itself provided a vehicle for addressing them. . . . Graduates put together what they had learned into practice by influencing others to register and vote, by assuming leading and supportive roles in local civil rights campaigns, and by joining existing organizations or establishing new ones to tackle community welfare needs.[45]

Lack of Support

While the Citizenship Schools led to the registration of hundreds of African American voters, the program often lacked the funds it needed to be fully successful. Journalists Mack T. Hines III and Dianne Reed explain:

> The Citizenship Schools never received the full support of the SCLC leadership. The reason is that Dr. King and the other SCLC ministerial leaders overlooked Septima Clark's potential to serve as a well-rounded leader of the organization. . . . Consequently the SCLC leadership failed to consistently provide Septima Clark with the resources needed to continuously conduct meaningful voter registration workshops.[46]

Despite this lack of support from the SCLC, Clark nonetheless was responsible for providing over one hundred teachers the training they needed to establish their own Citizenship Schools. She oversaw all the workshops, trained most of the new teachers, and spent time with the participants. She made sure that everyone was treated in a courteous and respectful manner. By 1970, Olson explains, "some ten thousand citizenship school teachers trained by her and her colleagues had taught more than one hundred thousand blacks to read and write and demand their rights of citizenship."[47] Furthermore, as Clark proudly stated in 1985, "from one end of the South to the other, if you look at black elected officials and the political leaders, you find people who had their first involvement in the training program of the citizenship school."[48]

Clark stayed with the SCLC until the early 1970s, at which time she retired at the age of seventy-two. She eventually returned to Charleston, South Carolina, where she became the first black woman to serve on the Charleston School Board, the same group that had dismissed her for her membership in the NAACP years earlier. In 1982 Clark was honored with the Palmetto Award, the highest honor given in South Carolina. The College of Charleston has since named its auditorium after her. She died in 1987 at the age of eighty-nine in a nursing home on Johns Island.

Dorothy Cotton (1930–   )

The second of four girls whose mother died early, Dorothy Cotton, born in the 1930s, was raised by her father, a laborer in a tobacco factory in Goldsboro, North Carolina. With the help of one of her teachers, she was able to attend Shaw University in Raleigh, North Carolina. She paid additional expenses by holding down three jobs while there.

Through one of those jobs, she met Wyatt T. Walker, a minister who later became a key figure in the SCLC. Her life as a civil rights activist began in the late 1950s when she was a graduate student in Petersburg, Virginia. She participated in picketing the local library to protest against segregation. She later moved to Atlanta, Georgia, where she began working for the SCLC. Cotton once stated, "The movement became my whole life."

Dorothy Cotton, like Septima Clark, was one of several people involved in the SCLC Citizenship Schools. In her role as teacher and coordinator, she helped train hundreds of blacks to vote and participate in political activities. In her classes she utilized singing as well as other lessons. To help teach reading, for example, she taught the students to sing the words as they spelled them, then a discussion would be held about what the words meant.

In the late 1980s Cotton became the director of student activities at Cornell University in Ithaca, New York, where she continued to hold workshops focusing on race relations, women's issues, and nonviolence.

Quoted in Phil McCombs. "Dorothy Cotton and the Lessons of Freedom: The SCLC Educator's Civil Rights Memories." *Washington Post*, January 18, 1988.

Dorothy Cotton was a teacher and coordinator for the SCLC Citizenship Schools.

Upon Clark's death, then governor Carroll Campbell of South Carolina lauded her as "a leading civil rights activist . . . a legendary educator, and humanitarian."[49] For six decades, Clark dedicated her life to improving the lives of her fellow African American citizens. Historian Karenna Gore Schiff summarizes: "Septima was a transformative teacher to thousands of blacks . . . who, touched by her influence, became the voters, the marchers, and the organizers of the civil rights movement."[50]

Chapter Four

The Women of the Montgomery Bus Boycott

While African Americans suffered discrimination in many aspects of segregated southern society, one of the most observable and humiliating forms of discrimination occurred on city buses. Blacks were treated like second-class citizens and demeaned on a daily basis; they were forced to sit in the back of the bus, enter by a back door, and taunted and cheated by white drivers. Blacks were also required to give up their seat on the bus if a white person needed a place to sit.

Segregation on city buses was challenged successfully in 1955 in the city of Montgomery, Alabama. After the arrest of a black woman for refusing to give up her seat for white passengers, blacks in Montgomery decided to boycott, or stop riding, the buses. They boycotted the buses for over a year, despite threats, firebombings of homes of prominent blacks, and the hardship of finding other ways to get to work. Finally the Supreme Court ruled that bus segregation would have to end in Montgomery.

Two women played instrumental roles in the 1955 Montgomery bus boycott: Jo Ann Robinson and Rosa Parks. While Martin Luther King Jr. received most of the historical credit for

A nearly empty bus shows the effectiveness of the Montgomery, Alabama, bus boycott. The boycott went on for more than a year, until the U.S. Supreme Court ruled bus segregation laws unconstitutional.

the boycott, it was these two women who sparked the protest and then helped organize and carry it out. The boycott was the first successful protest against white domination by significantly large numbers of ordinary black citizens.

Jo Ann Robinson

Jo Ann Gibson Robinson was born in Culloden, Georgia, the twelfth child of a farming family. She became the only one of the twelve children to finish college when she graduated from Georgia State College. After teaching in both California and Texas, Robinson moved to Montgomery, Alabama, in 1949 to teach at the all-black Alabama State College.

It was also in 1949 that Robinson boarded a Montgomery bus to take her to the airport. The bus was nearly empty when she boarded, so she took a seat in the white section. The bus driver immediately began yelling at her and raised his arm as if to hit her. "Get up from there! Get up from there!" he yelled. "I felt . . . like a dog,"[51] Robinson later reported.

She was not the only black to suffer such indignities on buses in the South. Segregation rules mandated that blacks sit in the back of the bus and were strictly enforced. If their seats were needed

Mary Fair Burks and the Women's Political Council

Mary Fair Burks was the cofounder of the Women's Political Council (WPC) of Montgomery, Alabama. Burks, the head of the English Department at Alabama State College, grew up in Montgomery and witnessed segregation firsthand. Burks described how she got involved in civil rights activism: "I was in my car just behind a bus when the traffic light turned green. As I started to accelerate, I saw a white woman attempting to get to the curb. The short of it was that after the woman stopped cursing me, I was arrested. . . . It was after this traumatic experience that I resolved to do something about segregation."[1]

As a result of this incident, in 1946 Burks formed the WPC for the purpose of fighting some of the problems blacks faced in the community as a result of segregation. In the initial meeting of the WPC, the forty women there decided to use a three-tier approach. Their first goal was to register as many black voters as possible; secondly, they would focus on protesting the many abuses that occurred against blacks on the city buses. Finally, the group wanted to educate high school students about democracy, while also teaching adults to read and write so they could pass the literacy requirements for voting. To accomplish the third goal, the women of the WPC sought to register and set an example. Despite the fact that many of the women had advanced college degrees, a number of them failed the heavily biased literacy tests. The group's biggest success would come with their role in the Montgomery bus boycott. Journalist Stewart Burns elaborates: "WPC was the largest, best organized and most assertive black civic organization in the Alabama capital."[2]

1. Quoted in Vicki L. Crawford, Jacqueline Anne Rouse, and Barbara Woods, eds. *Women in the Civil Rights Movement: Trailblazers and Torchbearers.* Bloomington: Indiana University Press, 1993, p. 78.
2. Quoted in Brenna Sanchez. "Mary Fair Burks."*Contemporary Black Biography*, January 1, 2004.

for white passengers, black riders were required to stand. In addition, blacks were required to pay for their fares at the front of the bus but then were forced to leave the bus and board through the back door. Often, bus drivers simply drove away before black passengers could enter the bus. Historian Lynne Olson elaborates: "The bus drivers, all of them white, were in the words of a white city commissioner, 'mean as rattlesnakes.' It was not unusual for them to drive past a stop where blacks were waiting, or to engage in the sport of driving off just as a black passenger, having paid her fare, was about to board through the back door."[52]

Challenging the Authorities

In part because of this incident, Robinson became a member of the Women's Political Council (WPC), a group formed by educator Mary Fair Burks in 1946 and made up of professional black women who worked in Montgomery. The group worked on voter registration and sought to make improvements to the black community. Robinson became president of the WPC in the early 1950s.

In May 1954 Robinson, on behalf of the WPC, sent a letter to the mayor of Montgomery about the continued abuses and harassment of blacks on the city buses. In the letter, Robinson wrote: "More and more of our people are already arranging with neighbors and friends to ride to keep from being insulted and humiliated by bus drivers."[53] She also informed the mayor that the black citizens of Montgomery might boycott the city buses if nothing was done to improve the situation. She pointed out that blacks made up about 90 percent of the riders, and the city's downtown stores benefited financially from this high percentage; a boycott could therefore be financially devastating. The mayor and city government ignored the warning, choosing not to improve the situation on the buses.

While city authorities refused to act, a group of people, including Robinson, black attorney Fred Gray, and E.D. Nixon of the National Association for the Advancement of Colored People (NAACP), began looking for a person who could serve as a test case to challenge bus segregation in the courts. The group thought they had found one in March 1955 when fifteen-year-old Claudette Colvin was arrested for not giving up her seat on a bus. It was soon discovered, however, that the young girl was pregnant and unwed. The NAACP realized that white lawyers could use the pregnancy to question the morality of Colvin, so they decided to wait and see if another candidate could be found. That candidate would be Rosa Parks.

Rosa Parks

Rosa McCauley was born in Tuskegee, Alabama, in 1913 and grew up on a small farm. She attended school at the Montgomery Industrial School for girls until she was a teenager; at that time she quit school and got a job as a maid to help support her sick mother. In 1932 she married Raymond Parks, completed her high school education, and attended a few classes at Alabama State College in Montgomery.

In a seminal moment in the civil rights movement, Rosa Parks is booked for refusing to give up her seat to a white passenger on a Montgomery bus on December 1, 1955.

Rosa Parks joined the NAACP in 1943. She served as the Montgomery chapter's youth adviser and as the organization's secretary. She typed letters on an old typewriter and called members to remind them of meetings and projects in the black community. She answered phones, handled mail, and sent out press releases. She also kept track of every complaint that flooded into the office concerning racial violence and discrimination. Parks spent many hours walking through the black community, asking for volunteers, and telling people about the kind of work the NAACP was doing.

In addition to working for the NAACP, Parks also held a variety of other jobs—everything from being a house cleaner to a seamstress. By 1955 she was working long hours at her sewing machine in the back room of the Fair Department Store in downtown Montgomery. On weekends she labored at home, sewing for white customers. One of her best customers was a white woman named Virginia Durr, a well-known civil rights activist in the Montgomery area.

In the spring of 1955, Durr got a phone call from Highlander Folk School leader Myles Horton asking if she knew anyone who could benefit from a scholarship to the school. The school, under the guidance of Septima Clark, taught citizenship classes and helped prepare attendees to become local leaders in their own communities. Durr immediately thought of Parks and raised the necessary money for Parks to travel to the school.

When Parks returned to Montgomery after her week at Highlander, she found it even harder to endure the bus segregation and other discriminatory laws that were in effect. She had spent the week living on an equal basis with whites, and it was difficult to return to a life where she was surrounded by prejudice and discrimination.

The Arrest

On Thursday, December 1, 1955, Parks boarded a bus in Montgomery, paid the fare, and took a seat in the first row behind the whites-only section. As more and more passengers boarded the bus, the front seats filled quickly, and soon a white passenger was left standing. The driver walked to the back of the bus and ordered Parks and her seatmates to move. There was only one white

Virginia Durr (1903–1999)

Virginia Durr, the daughter of a white Alabama family, was a former member of the Junior League, a charitable organization. Durr was anything but a stereotypical southern belle. She belonged, for instance, to two interracial groups: the United Church Women and the Southern Conference for Human Welfare, groups of southern liberals intent on abolishing the poll tax and working for desegregation. She and her husband, Clifford, a lawyer who represented many of Montgomery's poor blacks, were also supporters of the Highlander Folk School.

As a result of their support of the Highlander school and their efforts to end segregation, Virginia and her husband were targeted by Mississippi senator James Eastland, who claimed the Durrs were Communists. The Durrs were required to testify before Eastland's committee. As she took the stand, Virginia chose to give only her name, state that she was not a Communist, and then remain silent. She later stated: "This is not a proper exercise of Congressional powers—This is nothing but a kangaroo court. . . . I stand in utter and complete contempt of this committee."[1] Even though the charges were unfounded, the Durrs were rejected by the white community in Montgomery, and their children were taunted at school.

The rejection did not deter the Durrs. When Rosa Parks was arrested, for example, they were present at the jail and drove Parks home. During the boycott, Virginia drove boycotting black workers to and from their jobs and helped raise money for Parks, who had lost her job. Later, during other civil rights protests, the Durrs opened their home for civil rights workers. Their home became the hub for journalists, activists, historians, and others who were drawn to Montgomery during the Freedom Rides and the later Selma to Montgomery march. Upon her death in 1999, United Press International described Virginia Durr as "a southern rebel and granddaughter of slaveholders who battled as hard to overthrow white supremacy in the South as her grandfather fought to preserve it."[2]

Virginia Durr poses with (left to right) author William Styron, newsman Mike Wallace, and columnist Art Buchwald.

1. Quoted in Karenna Gore Schiff. *Lighting the Way: Nine Women Who Changed Modern America.* New York: Hyperion, 2005, p. 228.
2. "Virginia Durr Dead at 95." United Press International, February 24, 1999.

passenger, but all four black passengers were asked to move since segregation law forbade blacks from sitting in any row occupied by whites. The other black passengers did leave their seats, but Parks refused. She explained: "I had been pushed as far as I could stand to be pushed. I had decided that I would know once and for all what rights I had as a human being and a citizen. . . . I didn't give up my seat because I was tired. . . . No, the only tired I was, was tired of giving in."[54]

Charges were later made that Parks had acted on orders from the NAACP, but that simply was not the case. Journalist David Halberstam elaborates: "Later the stunned white leaders of Montgomery repeatedly charged that Parks's refusal was part of a carefully orchestrated plan on the part of the local NAACP, of which she was an officer. But that was not true; what she did represented one person's exhaustion with a system that dehumanized all black people."[55]

Parks insisted that she had no intention of getting arrested when she boarded the bus. Years afterward, she reflected on her thoughts that day. "When I got on the bus that evening I wasn't thinking about causing a revolution or anything of the kind," she explained. "I was thinking about my husband. . . . I was thinking about my back aching. . . . I told myself I wouldn't put up no fuss against them arresting me. . . . But I also knew I wasn't gonna give up my seat just because a white driver told me to; I'd already done that too many times."[56] It was only with the benefit of hindsight that Parks realized that her isolated act had helped spark the civil rights movement and the kind of protest that proved most productive. She had shown that the actions of individual citizens were important. In the late 1950s and the 1960s, individuals would again and again take action, small and large, in their own effort to stand up against the forces of segregation.

Parks was released on bail and that night, she and her husband met with the NAACP's Nixon and attorney Gray to discuss her upcoming trial. Nixon asked her if she would be a test case so that the NAACP could challenge bus segregation. Rosa was torn; she did not want to put her family at risk, but she also was sick and tired of the indignities she and other blacks faced on the buses. She finally stated, "If you think it will mean something to Montgomery and do some good, I'll be happy to go along with it."[57]

The Boycott

That same evening after meeting with Rosa Parks, Nixon and Gray contacted WPC leader Jo Ann Robinson about the possibility of boycotting the buses on Monday, December 5, the day of Parks's trial. Robinson immediately put the plans for such a boycott into effect; she and the women of the WPC, in fact, had already planned for such a contingency. She and other group members stayed up all night mimeographing more than thirty-five thousand handbills on the Alabama State University campus. In the years before printers and copiers, if an individual wanted copies of something, he or she had to use a machine called a mimeograph copier. This machine, a rotating ink-filled drum, was a low-cost printer that worked by forcing ink through a specially prepared stencil. One of these machines was used for creating the handbill, a small printed sheet that was passed around by hand. The women who created this handbill did so with great stealth; if the white authorities who controlled the university found out what they were doing, they would have been fired from their teaching positions.

The handbill that Robinson created read:

> Another Negro woman has been arrested and thrown into jail because she refused to get up out of her seat on the bus and give it to a white person. . . . Negroes have rights, too. . . . If we do not do something to stop these arrests, they will continue. The next time it may be you, or your daughter, or mother. The woman's case will come up on Monday. We are, therefore, asking every Negro to stay off the buses Monday in protest of the arrest and trial. Don't ride the buses to work, to town, to school, or anywhere on Monday.[58]

The notice was handed out at every black church in the Montgomery area. Hundreds of women worked through the night distributing the handbill to dozens of locations, including beauty shops, barbershops, factories, and storefronts. The word spread quickly. By the end of the weekend, nearly every black in the city of Montgomery knew about the plans for the boycott. Journalist Denise L. Berkhalter elaborates: "When Parks was arrested, Robinson and the

After Rosa Parks's arrest, a meeting at the Holt Street Baptist Church resulted in the creation of a new organization, the Montgomery Improvement Association, under the leadership of Martin Luther King Jr., who is shown here addressing the group.

three hundred–member Women's Political Council . . . provided the manpower and network needed to spread the word in the black community."[59]

The blacks of Montgomery eagerly waited for Monday morning. Robinson later spoke of that day:

Monday morning . . . I shall never forget because many of us had not gone to bed that night. . . . We had been up waiting for the first buses to pass to see if any riders were on them. It was a cold morning, cloudy, there was a threat of rain, and we were afraid that if it rained the people would get on the bus. But as the buses began to roll, and there were one or two on some of the buses, none on some of them, then we began to realize that the people were cooperating. . . . As a result, a very negligible number of riders rode that first day.[60]

In fact, over fifty thousand blacks chose not to ride the buses that day.

A Mass Meeting: The Boycott Continues

That day, while black passengers stayed off the buses, Parks had her day in court. She had been told by her lawyers that she was not to testify. The NAACP wanted her to be found guilty so they could appeal the conviction to a higher court, where the segregation laws could be changed. She was found guilty on December 5, 1955, of violating the city's segregation laws and ordered to pay a fine of ten dollars plus four dollars for court costs. Her attorneys immediately filed an appeal, which would eventually be heard by the U.S. Supreme Court.

That same night hundreds of blacks showed up at a mass meeting at Holt Street Baptist Church. The meeting had been convened to discuss the future of the boycott. As a result of Parks's arrest and the meeting at the church, a new organization was created, the Montgomery Improvement Association (MIA), under the leadership of Martin Luther King Jr., a young Montgomery minister. The group pledged to continue the boycott until bus segregation was ended in the city.

Prior to the bus incident and the mass meeting, King and many other black ministers in Montgomery had been reluctant to speak out against or fight segregation. Now they realized that if they did not respond to the mass outpouring of people supporting the boycott, they would lose their credibility with their congregations. King, when he accepted the leadership of the MIA, stated he would support the boycott but did not want to organize it. Fortunately, Robinson already had that covered.

The boycott was, in fact, organized and led by Robinson and other women. One such person was Irene West, a wealthy black resident of Montgomery. West, despite being close to eighty years old, drove every morning during the boycott. Taking out her Cadillac, she drove through the city, picking up people who needed a ride. Hundreds of white women also helped the boycott succeed by picking up their maids and other employees, whom they considered essential in the running of their homes.

As the boycott continued, all eighteen black cab companies agreed to pick up black passengers for low fares. When the police started arresting black cab drivers for not charging full price, the MIA asked for volunteer drivers. Robinson drove one car, while Parks served as the dispatcher for the other drivers. Service was provided from 5:30 in the morning until 12:30 at night; in all, thirty thousand blacks were transported each day to and from work. White drivers as well as black were harassed by the police, who handed out hundreds of tickets every day to people who were not violating any traffic laws.

Civil rights leaders Martin Luther King Jr. (second row, by window) and Ralph Abernathy (first row) ride with a white passenger on a newly desegregated Montgomery, Alabama, city bus in December 1956.

Despite the harassment, the blacks of Montgomery stayed off the buses for 381 days. The U.S. Supreme Court finally ruled on the case on November 13, 1956. The court upheld a federal district court ruling of June 4, 1956, that had stated that Alabama's segregation laws for buses were unconstitutional; that citizens were being deprived of their equal rights. This led to a city ordinance that allowed blacks to sit wherever they liked on buses. On December 21 blacks returned to the buses and sat according to their preference.

King later praised Robinson for her efforts. "Apparently indefatigable [untiring], she, perhaps, more than any other person, was active on every level of the protest. She took part in both the executive board and the strategy committee meetings. When the Montgomery Improvement Association newsletter was inaugurated a few months after the protest began, she became its editor."[61] Burks, founder of the WPC, also spoke of Robinson:

> Once [the boycott] was underway, nobody worked more diligently than she did as a representative of the board of the MIA and as a representative of the WPC. Although others had contemplated a boycott, it was due in large part to Jo Ann's unswerving belief that it could be accomplished, and her never-failing optimism that it would be accomplished, and her selflessness and unbounded energy that it was accomplished.[62]

Later Lives

Both Rosa and Raymond Parks lost their jobs because of the boycott. Unable to find work and not feeling safe in Montgomery, the couple eventually moved to Detroit, Michigan, where Rosa ended up working for twenty years as the receptionist in the Michigan office of U.S. Representative John Conyers. The couple also founded the Rosa and Raymond Parks Institute for Self-Development in 1987, a career counseling center for black youth. In 1988, at the Democratic National Convention in Atlanta, Georgia, Rosa Parks was introduced to the delegation by Jesse Jackson, a candidate for the Democratic presidential nomination and a civil rights activist. He called her "the mother of the civil rights movement."[63] Parks was later awarded the Presidential Medal of Freedom in 1996, the highest honor for civilians in the United States. Upon her death in 2005, Parks became the first woman to lie in honor in the U.S. Capitol rotunda. This honor was granted because of a Senate-passed resolution.

Robinson continued her teaching career after the successful boycott. She taught at Alabama State University in the 1960s, then briefly at Grambling College in Louisiana. She eventually moved to Los Angeles, California, where she worked as a teacher until the late 1970s. Thelma Glass, a former member of the WPC, praised Robinson: "In all my years working and living with civic and educational activities, I have never met a woman who was more courageous than Jo Ann Robinson."[64]

Chapter Five

Daisy Bates and School Desegregation

School segregation was a matter of great concern for civil rights activists. In the late nineteenth century, the Supreme Court ruled that as long as schools provided equality in education, separate schools for the races were legal. Schools for blacks, however, provided an inferior education, from inadequate buildings to poor funding.

In the early 1950s the National Association for the Advancement of Colored People (NAACP) found several test cases that could challenge the "separate but equal" decision of the court. These cases were consolidated into *Brown v. Board of Education*, a case heard before the Supreme Court in 1952 and 1953. The court handed down its decision on May 17, 1954, stating that separate, or segregated, schools were unconstitutional and that such schools were not equal. The court ordered the southern states to begin the process of integrating their schools.

Desegregation came slowly in the South. Arkansas had integrated a few of its schools in various locations, but little had been done in the state's capital, Little Rock. Arkansas NAACP president and civil rights activist Daisy Bates took it upon herself to

The NAACP attorneys who successfully argued *Brown v. Board of Education* before the Supreme Court. From left to right are George E.C. Hayes, Thurgood Marshall, and James Nabrit Jr., as they pose triumphantly before the Supreme Court Building.

lead the effort to desegregate Central High School in that city. She quickly became known as the adviser to the nine black students who were chosen to integrate the school. Her house was the official pickup and drop-off site for the students; it was also where the press gathered each day. Throughout the long ordeal, Bates was the students' counselor and protector. One of the students, Ernest Green, later stated: "She was a quarterback, the coach. We were the players."[65] Historians credit Bates's persistence in integrating Little Rock's Central High School with bringing the school desegregation issue to the forefront of public awareness.

Daisy Bates Fights for Civil Rights

Daisy Lee Gatson was born in Huttig, Arkansas, in 1914. While she was a baby, her mother was raped and killed by white men. Fearing for his life, her father ran away. Daisy was adopted and raised by Orlee and Susie Smith, friends of her family. Daisy did not find out about the murder of her mother until she was eight. Because the perpetrators had never been punished, Daisy nursed a hatred of whites for most of her life. Throughout her teenage years, she fantasized about revenge against the men who had killed her mother. Eventually, she would turn this hatred toward working to end the humiliation and discrimination that she and other blacks faced every day.

She met her future husband, Lucius Christopher (called L.C.) Bates when she was fifteen years old. He was twelve years older than Daisy and worked as an insurance agent and newspaper reporter. Daisy dated L.C. for twelve years before marrying him in 1941, although they began living together in the early 1930s. Shortly before the marriage, the couple moved to Little Rock, Arkansas, where L.C. started a newspaper, the *Arkansas State Press*. The paper offered local and national news to African Americans, with an emphasis on civil rights. Daisy Bates soon began writing articles and editorials for the paper that were highly critical of segregation.

Bates earned particularly negative criticism from the white community when she wrote an article about the death of a black soldier. She had witnessed the incident and also interviewed others who had been present. Her article focused on the prejudice and discrimination that had led to the shooting. She also brought attention to the fact that the soldier had been shot five times while lying on the ground. Yet the police had called the shooting justified.

Highly critical of what had occurred, Bates and her husband called on the black leaders of Little Rock to perform their own investigation; the Negro Citizens' Committee was formed and ruled that the police had acted unprofessionally. The committee sent its report to the mayor and also to the secretary of war, as well as President Franklin Roosevelt. Federal authorities eventually agreed that the shooting had not been justified. Charges were

69

Challenging College Segregation

In February 1956 twenty-six-year-old African American student Autherine Lucy, hoping to obtain her master's degree, was admitted to the University of Alabama. Lucy was met by a mob of whites who prevented her from entering the administration building. The unruly crowd threw eggs and other objects at her, while the white supremacist group the Ku Klux Klan burned a cross on the college lawn. Not to be deterred, Lucy went to classes escorted by the police. The stress on the young collegian, however, was phenomenal, and her health began to deteriorate. She was suspended from the university in her first semester, supposedly for her own protection. She was then reinstated, then expelled again, and once again reinstated. Finally, she had had enough; she withdrew from the school. Lucy was finally granted her degree from the University of Alabama in 1992.

Charlayne Hunter-Gault had a similar experience at the University of Georgia in 1961. She describes what happened: "On January 9, 1961, I walked onto the campus at the University of Georgia to begin registering for classes. . . . The officials at the university had been fighting for a year and half to keep me out. I was not socially, intellectually, or morally undesirable. I was Black. And no Black student had ever been admitted to the University . . . in its 176-year history." Hunter-Gault was nineteen at the time and suffered intimidation and threats during her tenure. Despite the difficulties, she graduated two years later, becoming one of the first two blacks to graduate from the University of Georgia.

Quoted in Bettye Collier-Thomas and V.P. Franklin, eds. *Sisters in the Struggle: African American Women in the Civil Rights–Black Power Movement*. New York: New York University Press, 2001, p. 75.

Autherine Lucy, the first African American to be admitted to the University of Alabama, is escorted by police to her classes in 1956.

later filed against one of the policemen, but a white grand jury in Little Rock dismissed the charges; no one was ever punished for the shooting.

Another article led to both L.C. and Daisy Bates being arrested in 1946 after their criticism of the handling of an incident involving striking mill workers who had been picketing a Southern Cotton Oil Mill plant for better wages. During a strike-breaking incident, several black protesters were arrested, found guilty of breaking the right-to-work law, and sentenced to a year in prison. Daisy wrote an editorial criticizing the judge, the jury, and the law. A month later she and her husband were arrested and charged with contempt of court. The judge sentenced them to ten days in jail; the charges were eventually overturned by an appeals court. These two incidents merely increased the couple's determination to continue their fight for civil rights.

By the early 1950s Little Rock government officials were beginning to make a few small changes. The Little Rock Zoo, for instance, began admitting black visitors, and a few downtown hotels were allowing organizations with black members to use their meeting rooms. Despite this relaxation of the segregation law, Daisy Bates felt that the city and state were not doing enough. She ran for and was elected president of the Arkansas NAACP in 1952. Due to low membership numbers, however, the organization was unable to accomplish anything of significance during the first few years of her presidency.

Bates Fights School Segregation

In 1954 the Supreme Court ruled in *Brown v. Board of Education* that school segregation was unconstitutional. As a result of the court decision, some states began integrating their public schools fairly quickly, but the majority of southern states delayed making any changes. Since the court had not definitely outlined when desegregation should take place, many state governments took no action. Bates learned in a meeting with Arkansas lawmakers in 1954 that the city of Little Rock would integrate slowly. Not satisfied with a plan to start with high school students in 1957 and gradually incorporate other grades over the next three years, Bates took action.

Disgusted with the slowness of the plan, Bates met with national NAACP leaders in late 1955. With their assistance, she helped organize thirty-three black students, from first grade to high school. All of the students applied at white schools; all were denied admission. Eventually, Bates and the NAACP filed a lawsuit in federal court charging the schools with discrimination. The federal judge, however, ruled that the Little Rock Board of Education was not violating the law, because it was moving at a reasonable speed toward integration. Other appeals were likewise denied. By the summer of 1957, Bates had become well known to the community, black and white, as a champion of black equality through her editorials and newspaper articles that were critical of discrimination and segregation practices. She was viewed by some as a heroine and by others as a troublemaker.

The Little Rock Nine

The admission of black students to all-white Central High School in Little Rock was scheduled to take place on September 3, 1957. During the summer preceding the school year, Superintendent of Schools Virgil T. Blossom chose nine black students to enter the all-white high school. These students would become known as the Little Rock Nine; they included Minnijean Brown, Elizabeth Eckford, Ernest Green, Thelma Mothershed, Melba Pattillo, Gloria Ray, Terrence Roberts, Jefferson Thomas, and Carlotta Walls.

Bates immediately began to meet with the group and counsel them, telling them that they could expect to encounter anger and probably violence from white students and others. One of the students, Pattillo, later wrote about her first meeting with Bates: "She seemed very calm and brave considering the caravans of segregationists said to be driving past her house and tossing firebombs and rocks through her windows. They saw her as their enemy."[66]

During this entire period, Bates had been under constant verbal and sometimes physical attack. Historian Linda Reed elaborates: "Daisy Bates will surely be remembered for her courage in withstanding verbal threats, verbal abuses, and physical danger in her efforts to make room for everyone within the framework of American democracy."[67] Bates was arrested on numerous occasions on trumped up charges. The Ku Klux Klan burned a number of crosses on her front lawn, despite the house being protected by friends and family. In one of the earliest attacks, a rock was thrown through her window. Bates wrote about the incident in her autobiography: "I threw myself to the floor. I was covered with shattered glass. . . . I reached for the rock lying in the middle of the floor. There was a note tied to it. . . . Scrawled in bold print were the words 'Stone this time. Dynamite next.'"[68]

During the middle of the school crisis, many of her critics had warned Bates that if she continued to fight for integration, they would destroy her livelihood; they followed through with this threat. White segregationists applied pressure to those who advertised in the Bateses' newspaper, resulting in a significant loss in circulation. Hundreds of white readers canceled their subscriptions; many blacks also canceled because they feared violent reprisals. By early 1958 the paper was on the verge of collapse, and in 1959 it ceased publication.

Daisy Bates meets with some of the Little Rock Nine at her home in 1957. She counseled them to be prepared for anger and probably violence from whites.

Barbara Johns (1935–1991)

In 1951 Barbara Johns was a junior at Robert R. Moton High School, a black school in Farmville, Virginia. She and her classmates were frustrated with the appalling conditions of the school they attended; many classes were held in shacks or old buses. In addition, the all-white school board prohibited the school's students from taking such courses as geometry, algebra, world history, and geography. Meanwhile, just a few miles away, sat a new white high school, complete with auditorium, cafeteria, and other amenities. Despite the proximity, the students at Moton could not attend this high school because of segregation.

Johns and a few of her friends decided to see if they could improve the conditions at their school. On the morning of April 23, 1951, they got the principal out of the school by making a false telephone call about students skipping school. Once that had been accomplished, Johns passed the word that there was a meeting in the assembly hall. Johns then took the stage, asked the teachers to leave, and told the students they needed to go on strike for better school accommodations. The students agreed; they refused to attend classes and surrounded the school carrying signs demanding better conditions.

When the school superintendent refused to meet their demands, Johns met with a representative of the NAACP named Oliver Hill. Hill and his partners agreed to take the students' case if their parents were willing to fight not only for a new school but for desegregation of the school district. The parents agreed, and the strike ended after two weeks. The case later became known as *Davis et al. v. County School Board of Prince Edward County*. The NAACP would eventually combine this case with several others, resulting in the *Brown v. Board of Education* case that went to the Supreme Court.

A number of last-minute attempts were made by Arkansas citizens and authorities to prevent the students' admission. On August 27, 1957, for instance, an injunction against integrating the school was filed by the Mothers' League, a group committed to maintaining segregation. Governor Orval E. Faubus appeared as a witness and supported the injunction, warning the court of potential race riots and violence if the black students were admitted. The judge ruled in favor of the Mothers' League. Three days later, on August 30, the NAACP asked the U.S. District Court to overrule the injunction. This was granted; the judge warned that no one should interfere with the students. In response, Faubus mobilized the Arkansas National Guard on September 2 and ordered guardsmen to surround the high school. That night Faubus gave a televised speech in which he warned: "Blood will run in the streets if Negro students should attempt to enter Central High School."[69]

A white crowd that stretched for two blocks was on hand the morning of September 3 to greet the nine students, who arrived at the school accompanied by Bates and several ministers. The National Guard refused to allow the students to enter the building. Journalist David Halberstam elaborates:

> As they [the students] approached the school, they were . . . threatened; when they finally reached the school, they were turned away by a National Guard captain, who said he was acting under the orders of Governor Faubus. . . . The confidence of the mob grew greater by the minute as it found that law enforcement officials were on its side. . . . Sensing this the ministers and children quickly retreated.[70]

Nearly three weeks passed before another attempt was made to integrate the school. Bates continued to meet with the students, offering support and encouragement. During that time President Dwight Eisenhower was in frequent contact with Governor Faubus. The president was furious that Faubus had defied the Supreme Court and had disobeyed the judge who had ordered that integration should proceed. After a meeting of the two men and another hearing, Faubus, realizing that he might be arrested, decided to remove the troops. The students would try again to enter the high school on Monday, September 23.

The nine students met at Bates's house that Monday morning. Bates gave the students an encouraging speech, as historian Halberstam explains: "She reminded the children again and again that they were doing this not for themselves but for others, some as yet unborn. They were now, like it or not, leaders in a moral struggle."[71]

Bates was in contact with the Little Rock Police, who promised to escort the students into the school. The police complied with their promise, sneaking the students in a side door while a large white crowd gathered outside. When the crowd learned that the students were inside the school, violence broke out. The police force was insufficient to control the level of violence; Blossom, for that reason, ordered the students home for their safety. They were escorted out a back entrance by the police and driven home.

Because Bates had kept the press informed, the event made the front pages of newspapers across the country. This led to outcries from concerned citizens, who implored the president to act. The students stayed home the next day and watched on television that night as Eisenhower announced that he was sending in federal troops. Over twelve hundred soldiers from the 101st Airborne Division arrived and took up positions around the high school. Bates was notified that the students could safely return to the school.

While not in direct communication with the president, Bates had nonetheless helped pressure him to take action. As Reed explains: "Daisy Bates played an important role in forcing the federal government to . . . act as the guarantor of rights. . . . The Little Rock crisis marked the first deployment of federal power in the post-Reconstruction South to enforce equal citizenship."[72]

The next morning, the students met at Bates's house and were driven to school by the soldiers. Each of the nine young people was given a personal escort who stayed with the student throughout the day. Bates describes the scene:

> The nine Negro pupils marched solemnly through the doors of Central High School, surrounded by twenty-two soldiers. An Army helicopter circled overhead. Around the massive brick schoolhouse, 350 paratroopers stood grimly at attention. Scores of reporters, photographers, and television cameramen made a mad dash for telephones, typewriters, and television studios, and within minutes a world that had been holding its breath learned that the nine pupils . . . had finally entered the never-never land.[73]

By the first of October, the situation had calmed enough that the Arkansas National Guard was able to replace the soldiers. Even with federal orders to protect the children, the National

Soldiers escort the Little Rock Nine students into Central High School. President Eisenhower sent the troops to Little Rock after Arkansas governor Orval Faubus refused to obey a court order to desegregate the school.

Guard refused to do so. Bates kept careful records of each abusive incident and in November took the material to Blossom. Blossom thought Bates was exaggerating and advised her to take the problem to the National Guard. She spoke to the commander of the troops, as well as city and state government officials, but nothing was done. Bates continued not only to write about the problems the students were having but to speak out about them. Finally, a guardsman was assigned to each student. This, however, did not deter many of the white students from continuing their harassment and abuse of the blacks.

After a tumultuous and violent year, however, the one senior among the nine students graduated from Central High School in the spring of 1958. He was the first black to do so. Despite the courage and success of the Little Rock Nine, integration came slowly to the city; by 1962 only eighty black students were attending white schools.

Afterward

During the summer of 1958, Bates and the nine students were frequently praised by the national press. They dined with the governor of New York and were also given a private tour of the White House. On July 11, 1958, Bates and the students were given the NAACP's most prestigious award, the Spingarn Medal.

Bates continued her work for the NAACP, as well as SCLC. In the 1960s President John Kennedy appointed her to the Democratic National Committee; she also served as an adviser to President Lyndon Johnson on his antipoverty campaign. After her husband's death in 1980, she revived the newspaper, the *State Press*.

Daisy Bates watches Arkansas governor Orval Faubus give his reasons for not following a federal court order to desegregate Little Rock schools. Bates played an important role in pressuring the federal government to enforce civil rights laws.

Marian Wright Edelman (1939–   )

Born in South Carolina in 1939, Marian Wright Edelman attended Spelman College and then traveled the world on a scholarship before returning to the United States. In the 1960s Edelman went to Mississippi to help with voter registration, and she was arrested for her efforts. Her arrest and the injustice she witnessed compelled her to attend Yale Law School. When she graduated, she returned to Mississippi and became the first African American woman to be admitted to that state's bar. She took a job working for the NAACP's Legal Defense and Education Fund. Her main focus was defending civil rights demonstrators and challenging school segregation.

In 1968 she moved to Washington, D.C., and provided legal assistance to the Poor People's Campaign, an effort to publicize the plight of the poor. She created an organization that later became the Children's Defense Fund, a group intent on protecting and assisting children across the country. To provide the needed assistance, the organization has encouraged the passage of laws that provide children with health care and education as well as protection from abuse and neglect. For her work with children, Edelman was awarded the Presidential Medal of Freedom in 2000.

Through the Children's Defense Fund, Edelman helped awaken the country to the fact that children have rights. The editors of *Ladies' Home Journal* summarize: "She has done more to shape national policy on such issues as infant mortality, day care, child abuse, and teenage pregnancy than probably any legislator who has ever worked in Washington."

Quoted in Kevin Markey. *One Hundred Most Important Women of the Twentieth Century*. Des Moines, IA: Meredith, 1998, p. 23.

She again focused on civil rights issues and kept the paper going until 1987. At that time she suffered a stroke, and she struggled with finances the remainder of her life.

Bates died on November 4, 1999. After her death one of the streets passing Central High School was renamed Daisy Bates Drive. Arkansas also became the first state to honor an African American by proclaiming the third Monday of February a state holiday in her honor and by allowing her coffin to lie in state at the capitol in Little Rock, an honor ordinarily reserved for politicians.

Chapter Six

Ella Baker, the Spiritual Leader of the Student Nonviolent Coordinating Committee

Ella Baker is often overlooked as a civil rights leader because she worked for several organizations with strong male leaders who received most of the credit in the fight for equality. From the 1930s until her death in 1986, in fact, Baker participated in over thirty different organizations and civil rights campaigns. She fought for civil rights on the front lines for over half a century.

In an interview on National Public Radio in 2003, one of Baker's biographers, Barbara Ransby, spoke glowingly of Baker:

> She was involved in the Black Freedom Movement for some fifty years, was a pivotal person at every turn in the move-

ment's history from Harlem [New York] in the 1930s where she was involved in the Cooperative Movement, worked in the trenches of the NAACP [National Association for the Advancement of Colored People] in the 1940s, worked alongside [Martin Luther] King [Jr.] in the 1950s in Atlanta, [Georgia,] and then was really the inspiration and intellectual mentor to many of the young people who formed the Student Nonviolent Coordinating Committee [SNCC] in the 1960s.[74]

The SNCC was established in 1960 by students who had been involved in the lunch counter sit-ins in the South. Hundreds of students, black and white, had participated in challenging segregation at all-white lunch counters and had succeeded in integrating many of the restaurants. Because of their success, the Southern Christian Leadership Conference (SCLC), led by King, was interested in having the students join that organization. Baker encouraged the students to form an independent organization and continue their protests and other forms of direct and nonviolent action against segregation. In part because of Baker's counsel, the SNCC would go on to play a prominent role in voter registration and civil rights protests throughout the South in the years that followed.

Baker, through her various grassroots efforts, nurtured a generation of activists to carry forward the civil rights movement. Her leadership often went unnoticed, but the collective of her contributions had an undeniable and lasting impact. Historian Howard Zinn once described Baker as "moving silently through the protest movements in the South doing the things the famous men didn't have time to do."[75] Journalist Marilyn Bordwell DeLaure elaborates further: "Baker brought people together, cultivated a sense of community through identification, made space for local leadership to emerge, and taught new generations of activists how to organize and carry on the struggle."[76]

Early Years

Ella Josephine Baker was born in Norfolk, Virginia, in 1903 and grew up in Littleton, North Carolina. She had little direct contact with whites during her childhood. Instead she witnessed a lot of intelligent and determined blacks working toward building a strong community. She saw blacks striving for economic independence and self-sufficiency: the creation of black businesses with blacks helping blacks wherever they turned. Her parents stressed the importance of economic self-sufficiency and racial pride. Baker describes the importance of her upbringing: "The sense of community was pervasive [present everywhere] in the black community as a whole. . . . I think these are the things that helped to strengthen my concept about the need for people to have a sense of their own values, and their own strengths."[77]

Ella Baker, a lifelong civil rights activist, was called the spiritual leader of the Student Nonviolent Coordinating Committee.

Ella's mother, Georgianna Baker, was active in the black Baptist women's missionary movement of the early 1900s. Ella and her siblings often accompanied their mother to the meetings of this group; there they witnessed firsthand the work that black women were doing to help the poor, sick, and elderly.

After graduating from Shaw University in Raleigh, North Carolina, in 1927, Baker moved to New York City. One of the few occupations available to educated blacks at the time was teaching. Yet Baker turned down teaching jobs, preferring instead to work several low-paying jobs in various civil rights organizations. DeLaure elaborates: "She was a strong, assertive woman unafraid of speaking her mind. . . . [She embraced] an itinerant [traveling] and financially uncertain life of activism rather than choosing the respectable stable job of being a teacher."[78]

Living in Harlem, Baker was astounded by the poverty and hunger she saw in the area. She saw people living in dilapidated shacks without running water or basic sanitation. Hundreds of blacks went hungry due to lack of money to buy the most basic kinds of food. Baker quickly immersed herself in some of the political activities there. She protested the unfair treatment of black domestic workers, for instance, and helped launch the Young Negroes Cooperative League, a group whose actions were dedicated to improving the economic strength of blacks in Harlem. These workers were employed by some of the richest people in the New York area yet were paid very little and had to endure long hours and difficult labor. She also began working for a government program that helped promote literacy among the poor workers of New York City.

During the 1930s Baker worked for the Workers' Education Project of the Works Progress Administration (WPA) of the federal government. The WPA employed millions of unskilled workers to build roads and other projects, helped feed children, and distributed food and clothing. The Workers' Education Project focused on literacy and providing education opportunities for all citizens. Baker offered courses and workshops throughout the Harlem area aimed at educating blacks so they could obtain better-paying jobs. She was also associated with the Harlem branch of the Young Women's Christian Association (YWCA) and met its leader, civil rights activist Dorothy Height. Height and other female friends helped mold Baker into the ardent activist she was already becoming.

Field Director

Because of the experience Baker had obtained in Harlem and else-where, she was offered a position in the NAACP, the leading civil rights organization of the time. Baker was named the NAACP field director in 1940. While primarily focused on legal issues, during the 1940s the NAACP also pushed for a federal antilynching law and an end to state-mandated segregation. The 1940s also saw the NAACP dramatically increase its membership.

Baker was the perfect person for the job. One of her great-est gifts was her ability to organize people. During her years as field secretary for the NAACP, she traveled throughout the South. She organized youth chapters everywhere she went. Baker had an uncanny ability to communicate with people on their own level. Never condescending, she treated young people as intelligent in-dividuals who had much to offer the NAACP.

On the road for four to five months at a time, Baker also spoke to local NAACP chapters and helped those groups increase their membership. She also encouraged these local groups to focus on segregation problems in their towns and cities. She made con-tact with many people during her travels and often stayed in their homes as she moved from place to place. Through these contacts, Baker earned the trust of hundreds of people. By do-ing so she formed an extensive network of friendships upon which she would later draw. Historians Bettye Collier-Thomas and V.P. Franklin elaborate: "Her travels throughout the South in the 1940s as field secretary for the NAACP provided her with the personal knowledge needed for organizing the black work-ing class."[79] During that period, Baker met and talked with thou-sands of ordinary black citizens, male and female. Unlike other organizers, who tended to talk down to rural Southerners, she treated everyone with respect. As a result, she formed friendships wherever she went and learned what these individuals wanted in terms of civil rights and equality. These relationships would later provide her with a core group of people who could form a mass movement.

Baker eventually became the NAACP director of branches. In this position Baker became the highest-ranking female officer in the organization. It was her task to supervise field secretaries and coordinate local group activities with the goals of the national

Lillian Smith (1897–1966)

Lillian Eugenia Smith, a white southern writer, was a vocal critic of segregation and prejudice against African Americans for most of her life. Through her writings and friendships with black women, she became a loud voice of opposition to racism in the South. As the co-owner of the magazine the *South Today*, Smith printed the work of black women and also authored numerous articles and editorials critical of racial injustice. She then turned to writing books. Her best-selling novel *Strange Fruit*, published in 1944, was the story of an ill-fated love affair between an educated black woman and a young white man. The book was banned in various cities in the United States but eventually sold over 3 million copies and was translated into sixteen languages. The book was condemned throughout the South.

The success of this book provided Smith with financial independence, and she devoted the remainder of her life to supporting civil rights through her writing. Her second major book was *Killers of the Dream*, published in 1949. In the book, she analyzed her upbringing in a land of segregation. Her final book, *Our Faces, Our Words* (1965), was a pictorial essay about the civil rights movement.

She was an early and active member of the NAACP, the Congress of Racial Equality, and the SNCC. Like Ella Baker, Smith was committed to working wherever she was needed in an effort to end discrimination. Historian Lynne Olson elaborates on Smith's commitment to civil rights: "No Southern white woman was more liberal on racial issues . . . than Lillian Smith . . . who . . . ventured forth to call for the end of segregation at a time when other white Southern liberals still supported it."

Lynne Olson. *Freedom's Daughters: The Unsung Heroines of the Civil Rights Movement from 1830 to 1970.* New York: Simon and Schuster, 2001, p. 64.

Southern author Lillian Smith was a vocal critic of segregation and racial prejudice.

organization. She helped individual branch offices mount local campaigns in protest against segregation. With the NAACP national office primarily focusing on legal issues, she also encouraged the local offices to report any legal case that might interest the NAACP legal team.

The NAACP's reliance on legal tactics such as lawsuits to fight discrimination, however, frustrated Baker, who preferred more direct action, such as marches and protests. She also became dissatisfied with the NAACP's focus on increasing membership rather than addressing local issues, such as police brutality, school segregation, or other acts of discrimination. She wanted the organization to help empower people to take action on their own behalf. Frustrated with the organization, in 1946 she quit her job as field director, although she did remain president of the New York branch of the organization.

Working for the SCLC

After leaving the NAACP, Baker cofounded In Friendship, an organization that offered financial support for blacks who were actively fighting for civil rights. The group was dedicated to helping those who were suffering economic reprisals because of their fight against segregation. Those who spoke out against discrimination frequently were fired from their jobs; some were evicted from their homes. In Friendship's efforts were primarily restricted to the New York area and never became national in scope.

In the 1950s Baker headed south to help with the formation and organization of the SCLC. The SCLC was founded in January 1957 by activist King and a number of other southern black ministers. The organization's primary purpose was to coordinate and support nonviolent forms of direct action, such as boycotts. Baker became that organization's first full-time staff member. She was asked to organize the SCLC's Crusade for Citizenship, a series of citizen education programs designed to promote voter registration. She managed to organize church rallies in twenty-two cities, but there was no follow-up to the rallies from the SCLC leadership. The SCLC ministers were more focused, at that time, on their own churches and ministries and did not want to take the time to recruit voters or teach them how to vote. And so the plan for local registration never got off the ground.

The failure of the ministers to follow through with voter registration was but one example of Baker's frustration with the leadership. Thus, Baker's years in the SCLC were not without conflict. She frequently challenged the male leadership and male dominance within that organization and others. While she respected King, the creator and leader of the SCLC, she also had profound differences of opinion with him that she was not hesitant about voicing.

Baker believed that national leaders should draw their strength from ordinary people, not from the media or powerful financial backers, as King seemed to do at times. DeLaure elaborates: "In her grassroots organizing work, she eschewed the charismatic orator model of social movement leadership, seeking [instead] to empower ordinary people [to become leaders]."[80] Baker once stated: "I have always thought what is needed is the development of people who are interested not in being leaders as much as in developing leadership among other people."[81]

Ella Baker (second from right), seen here at an NAACP meeting, became the highest-ranking female member in that organization.

Gloria Richardson and the Cambridge Movement

Gloria Richardson grew up in Cambridge, Maryland. Although African Americans who lived there had been given the vote in the nineteenth century, blatant racism in Cambridge prevented true equality and kept most blacks from voting. Blacks also still suffered discrimination in education, jobs, housing, and medical care. The majority of African Americans in the city were poor and worked in inhumane workhouses. Most homes did not have indoor plumbing. These conditions caused a deep resentment among black Cambridge residents.

In 1962 Richardson, a graduate of Howard University, helped organize the Cambridge Nonviolent Action Committee, a group dedicated to desegregating public accommodations, increasing voter registration, and ousting several segregationist politicians. Despite the group's efforts, segregation policies actually worsened. In protest, the committee initiated a number of demonstrations that resulted in massive arrests, including that of Richardson, her mother, and her daughter. Over sixty people were arrested on a single day in March 1963.

Violence broke out in Cambridge as a result of these arrests. The city erupted in shootings, arson, and bomb threats. Within a few days the minority sections of the city were sealed off with roadblocks manned by Maryland state troopers. Martial law was imposed. A committee was finally convened in the nation's capital that included, among others, Richardson, Attorney General Robert Kennedy, and Cambridge mayor Calvin Mowbray. At this meeting the Treaty of Cambridge was signed, ending the violence and calling for a complete overhaul of the city's race relations. Despite the treaty, the town remained segregated.

Richardson was praised for her leadership and role in the Cambridge Movement. Called "the Lady General of Civil Rights" by *Ebony* magazine, Richardson, like Ella Baker, did not hesitate to take action when it was required.

Quoted in Bettye Collier-Thomas and V.P. Franklin, eds. *Sisters in the Struggle: African American Women in the Civil Rights–Black Power Movement*. New York: New York University Press, 2001, p. 187.

(Left to right, seated) Gloria Richardson, Attorney General Robert Kennedy, and Cambridge mayor Calvin Mowbray announce the signing of the Treaty of Cambridge.

Baker also was frustrated that the ministers who were in charge of the SCLC were apparently more interested in making King a national icon than they were in doing actual work for voter registration. She stated:

> I have always felt it was a handicap for oppressed people to depend so largely upon a leader, because unfortunately in our culture, the charismatic leader usually becomes a leader because he has found a spot in the public limelight. . . . There is also the danger in our culture that because a person is called upon to give public statements and is acclaimed by the established, such a person gets to the point of believing that he is the movement. Such people get so involved with playing the game . . . that they . . . don't do the work of actually organizing people.[82]

Some SCLC insiders and historians believe that King treated Baker more like a secretary than an organizer. They claim that Baker was never given credit for the work she did and that King often refused to take her calls. He and the other ministers seldom listened to her advice about grassroots organizing. Her suggestions, for instance, for greater emphasis on local organizing were largely ignored. Baker stated: "I knew from the beginning that as a woman, an older woman, in a group of ministers who are accustomed to having women largely as supporters, there was no place for me to have come into a leadership role."[83]

And yet Baker led in many different ways. She led by example and always advocated for equality, pushed for inclusion of all people in the civil rights movement, encouraged others to join the movement, and treated others with respect and appreciation. In addition, Baker led through her ability to organize various groups of people to fight for an end to discrimination in both small and large ways.

The *Fundi*

From her position within the SCLC, Baker watched with great interest as the student sit-ins at lunch counters began in 1960. These protests, undertaken by college students, challenged all-white lunch counters and restaurants. Black students sat down at the counters and refused to leave until they were served. The movement spread throughout the South and succeeded in integrating several department store lunch counters.

Baker worried, however, that the various groups of young people were disconnected and unorganized. It was for that reason that she conceived and arranged a youth conference at Shaw University between April 16 and 18, 1960. Ransby elaborates: "Her intention was to help the students consolidate their initial victories and make linkages with one another."[84] Over two hundred students responded to Baker's notice and attended the meeting.

The SCLC wanted the students to join their organization and form a student wing. In her keynote address to the students, Baker encouraged the students to remain independent instead. DeLaure elaborates: "She wanted to preserve the radical spirit and energy of the sit-ins and feared the students getting bogged down under the bureaucratic structure of existing organizations."[85] Baker had grown quite discouraged with the major civil rights groups and their slow pace of change and accomplishment. Most of the groups were content with verbal challenges; Baker felt more direct action, like the sit-ins, was needed. Thus, she encouraged the students to form their own independent organization instead of joining the SCLC or other groups.

In large part because of Baker's advice, the students formed the SNCC and declared themselves independent of any established civil rights group. They promised to dedicate themselves to direct action, such as protests and demonstrations. The SNCC quickly became a leading civil rights organization as the students began working on voter registration and other issues. In doing so, the student organization moved to the forefront of the civil rights movement; it was the only group that was out in the community, actively working with masses of black people to make positive changes.

Baker eventually left the SCLC and became the primary mentor and adviser to the SNCC. Civil rights activist and SNCC leader John Lewis considered Baker "the spiritual mother of SNCC."[86] Inspired by Baker's words and philosophy, many of the young SNCC leaders modeled themselves after her. They followed her principles of grassroots action. Baker elaborates: "My sense of it has always been to get people to understand that in the long run they themselves are the only protection they have against violence

Ella Baker speaks at a news conference in 1968. Baker became known
as the *Fundi,* a Swahili word for a person who passes on his or her
skills to the next generation.

or injustice. . . . People have to be made to understand that they
cannot look for salvation anywhere but to themselves."[87] She advocated a form of group-centered leadership. She believed that
a leader was only a facilitator, someone who could bring out the
potential in others. Furthermore, she thought that it was the thousands of ordinary people marching and protesting that helped
make the civil rights movement a success.

Diane Nash and the Nashville Student Movement

Diane Nash played a crucial leadership role during the civil rights movement. A Northerner by birth, Nash went south to attend Fisk University in Nashville, Tennessee, where she was immediately confronted with racism. Appalled by what she experienced, she began attending workshops focused on nonviolent forms of protest.

Nash became a prominent member of the Nashville Student Movement and played a pivotal role during the 1960 lunch counter sitins that swept the South. Journalist David Halberstam explains Nash's leadership role: "Whatever it was that needed to be done, she just did it. The leader had to be a person who made good decisions under terrible pressure. Like it or not, she was that person."[1] After a confrontation with the mayor on the courthouse steps, Nash and the students were successful in desegregating a number of Nashville lunch counters.

Nash also played a critical role during the May 1961 Freedom Rides that challenged interstate bus segregation. When violence stopped the original riders, the Nashville contingent of the SNCC stepped in. Nash spoke for the students about the reason for continuing the rides: "I strongly felt that the future of the [civil rights] movement was going to be cut short if the Freedom Ride had been stopped as a result of violence. The impression would have been that whenever a movement starts, all you have to do is attack it with massive violence and the blacks will stop."[2]

Nash took on the job of coordinating the group's participation in the rides. She oversaw the recruitment of students to take up the ride, garnered support from other civil rights organizations, and became the liaison between the students and the press. When the riders were arrested in Jackson, Mississippi, Nash also kept track of each person that was sent to prison. As the first riders disappeared into notorious Parchman Penitentiary, Nash sent out emergency calls for more riders. In all, over three hundred individuals responded to Nash's call. The Freedom Rides resulted in the integration of all interstate buses and bus facilities.

1. David Halberstam. *The Children*. New York: Fawcett, 1998, p. 144.
2. Quoted in Henry Hampton and Steve Fayer. *Voices of Freedom: An Oral History of the Civil Rights Movement from the 1950s through the 1980s*. New York: Bantam, 1990, p. 82.

In her role as the SNCC adviser, Baker met frequently with the student leaders. She also drafted many of the organization's early documents and was on hand to advise the young people on direct action strategy and goals. Lewis, one of those leaders, elaborates: "Baker, herself, praised our success so far but warned that our work had just begun. Integrating lunch counters in stores already patronized by blacks was one thing. Breaking down barriers in areas as racially and culturally entrenched as voting rights, education, and the workplace was going to be much tougher."[88] Because of her endeavors to cultivate leadership in others rather than be a leader herself, Baker came to be called the *Fundi*. It was SNCC member Robert Parrish Moses who first called Baker the *Fundi*. *Fundi* is a Swahali word for a person who passes on one's skills to future generations.

Later Life

While still continuing her work with the SNCC, in 1964 Baker also helped establish the Mississippi Freedom Democratic Party. Baker, in fact, was the keynote speaker at the party's first convention in April 1964. This party, made up of blacks, challenged the all-white delegation at the Democratic National Convention held in Atlantic City, New Jersey, in 1964. Although the party was unsuccessful in its attempt to be seated, the Democratic Party was forced to look at making significant changes for future selection of delegates so as to be inclusive of both blacks and whites. At the time, the Democratic Party was primarily run and controlled by white Southerners. Herb Boyd elaborates: "Miss Baker spoke directly to the way the Democrats and the entire nation contributed to the sustenance of white supremacy in Mississippi."[89]

Baker remained active in civil rights well into her eighties. She campaigned for liberation in Africa and continued to work for equality in the United States. Wherever she found a cause to fight for or a group to organize, Baker was there, offering her ability to mobilize and inspire people of all generations.

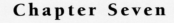

Chapter Seven

Fannie Lou Hamer and the Mississippi Freedom Democratic Party

The black women of Mississippi did not take a backseat to anybody in their determination to end segregation. They were out front, leading voter registration drives, forming a new political party, and helping create a grassroots revolution that eventually led to thousands of blacks becoming civil rights activists. Leading the way was former sharecropper Fannie Lou Hamer. Professor Mamie E. Locke describes Hamer: "She was one of those everyday kinds of people who stood firm in their beliefs and became role models for many. She became a symbol of the struggle for survival in a racist, hostile environment."[90]

A Sharecropper's Life

Fannie Lou Townsend, the youngest of twenty children, was born in 1917 and raised in Mississippi. Her parents were sharecroppers. Sharecropping was a system whereby workers, usually black, were allowed to live on a plantation in return for working the land. When the crop was harvested, they split the profits with the white plantation owner. Sharecroppers were required to pay for the seeds and fertilizer out of their half of the proceeds, leaving most of them in constant debt. It was a hard way to make a living; sharecroppers were usually born poor and died poor.

As part of the sharecropping tradition, Fannie Lou started working in the cotton fields at the age of six. She eventually married another sharecropper, Perry "Pap" Hamer. The couple lived in a small shack on a cotton plantation near Ruleville, Mississippi. For nearly twenty years, Hamer worked on this plantation.

Prior to 1962 Hamer had never heard of the civil rights movement. She attended her first civil rights rally in that year after hearing about the meeting at church. Members of the Student Nonviolent Coordinating Committee (SNCC) were in town hoping to recruit local blacks and spur an interest in voter registration. At the rally Hamer listened closely to what the speakers were saying. "Until then," she later stated, "I didn't know that Negroes could register and vote."[91] So impressed with what the young people from the SNCC were saying about her rights as a citizen, Hamer volunteered to be among seventeen blacks who would try to register to vote at the county seat of Indianola, Mississippi.

Registering to Vote

On August 31, 1962, Hamer and the other volunteers rode a bus to Indianola, where they took the literacy test that was required in order to vote in Mississippi. She and the others, however, failed the test and were thus unable to register. Hamer vowed to return time and again until she passed the test.

Hamer lost her job and home because of this attempt to register to vote. When she returned home, the owner of the plantation where Hamer worked told her that if she was going to try to register to vote, she would have to get off his land. Hamer refused to back down, and she was fired from her job; she was also evicted from her home. While her husband stayed behind to help finish the harvest, Hamer left the same day, staying that night with friends. From that day forward, she and her family were constantly threatened and harassed by whites.

Despite the threats, Hamer fully committed herself to civil rights activism. Because of her determination to register and her enthusiasm for fighting racism, Hamer was hired by the SNCC to work with people in the Mississippi delta, the area where she lived. She soon became a major voice in the South. Throughout the fall of 1962, she participated in movement-sponsored activities. Civil rights activist John Lewis elaborates: "From that sum-

Fannie Lou Hamer was born into a Mississippi sharecropper's family in 1917. Her steadfastness in the fight for civil rights served as a model for many.

mer on Fannie Lou became a tireless voice for our cause, putting herself out front as an organizer, a speaker . . . always an outspoken image of a poor, black woman who was simply out of patience. . . . Without her and hundreds of women like her, we would never have been able to achieve what we did."[92]

The Winona Incident

As part of her continuing civil rights activism, Hamer attended a Citizenship School program in Charleston, South Carolina. On June 9, 1963, Hamer, Annell Ponder, June Johnson, and four others were on their way home to Greenwood, Mississippi, on a Trailways bus. Their bus stopped in Winona, Mississippi, and the group walked into the white section of the depot waiting room. There they were approached by several police officers who ordered them to leave the area. When the women refused to do so, they were arrested.

Once at the Winona jail, the women were violently beaten while being questioned. Johnson, a sixteen-year-old, for instance, was hit on the back of the head with a nightstick; Ponder was repeatedly knocked to the floor and emerged from her questioning bloody and bruised. While the other women were being beaten, Hamer overheard the policemen talking about throwing their dead bodies into the Big Black River, where they would never be found.

Hamer describes what happened next: "Three white men came into my room. One was a state highway policeman. . . . They said they were going to make me wish I was dead."[93] The policemen gave a black prisoner a blackjack, a leather-covered club, and told him to beat Hamer. She elaborated: "The Negro beat me until he was exhausted . . . then the second Negro was given the blackjack . . . then the white man started to beat me in the head."[94] Hamer suffered permanent kidney damage and a blood clot that made her blind in the left eye. Historian Taylor Branch elaborates: "Hamer was beaten until the fingers protecting her head were blue and the skin on her back swelled up hard as a bone."[95]

Fortunately, the group had left a detailed itinerary before they left on the bus so that other civil rights activists would know where they were. When the group did not arrive in Greenwood, their colleagues began making phone calls and finally located the women in Winona. Lawrence Guyot, an SNCC member, drove to the jail and was promptly arrested and beaten. Eventually, two Southern Christian Leadership Conference (SCLC) officials were able to arrange for the prisoners' release. Historian Lynne Olson elaborates: "The two SCLC officials tried to hide their dismay at the shocking appearance of Hamer, Ponder, Johnson, and Guyot. Their eyes were blackened, swollen, and bloodshot; their faces and bodies were covered with huge dark bruises; they could barely speak."[96]

If the authorities in Mississippi believed that such beatings and arrests would stop Hamer and the other civil rights activists, they were very wrong. In June 1964, for instance, Hamer stated: "We're tired of all this beatin', we're tired of takin' this. It's been a hundred years [since the Emancipation Proclamation freeing the slaves] and we're still bein' beaten and shot at, crosses are still being burned because we want to vote. But I'm goin' to stay in Mississippi and if they shoot me down, I'll be buried here."[97]

Working for COFO

By late 1963 Hamer had also become a major figure in the Council of Federated Organizations (COFO). This was the activist arm of an alliance between the SNCC, National Association for the Advancement of Colored People (NAACP), and the Congress of Racial Equality. These groups had come together to help blacks in Mississippi register to vote.

On behalf of COFO, Hamer was sent to Washington, D.C., where she spoke at the National Theater on June 8, 1964. She described the situation in Mississippi to a panel of prominent Americans; she spoke of the violence and intimidation blacks faced every day in that state. She told the group about the violence she had encountered in the Winona jail and watched the shocked expressions on their faces as they heard her story.

Then she cried as she spoke about Mississippi's inhumane sterilization practices. Hamer described how she had gone into the hospital in 1961 for the removal of a cyst, only to wake up and find that the doctors had performed a hysterectomy, the removal of her uterus, without her knowledge. She furthermore recounted that six out of ten black women who entered the hospital were sterilized and rendered incapable of giving birth. Hamer explained that whites hoped by doing this to limit the number of black children born in Mississippi.

Amelia Boynton and Selma, Alabama

Amelia Boynton was a local Alabama civil rights activist who played a critical role in involving the SNCC and the SCLC in the politics of Selma, Alabama. Like Fannie Lou Hamer in Mississippi, Boynton worked efficiently at the local level in Alabama. She was, for instance, instrumental in persuading the SNCC to make Selma, an outpost of white supremacy, a center of protest activity for voter registration. As early as the 1930s, Amelia and Sam Boynton became active in the Dallas County Voters League, working to get blacks registered to vote. Despite their efforts, only 180 blacks in the county were registered by 1963 due to barriers thrown up by the city, county, and state.

Boynton also formally invited civil rights leader Martin Luther King Jr. to make Selma a major site for the SCLC's stalled voting rights campaign. In January 1965 Boynton was finally successful in persuading King to make Selma his next big campaign stop. Her insurance agency later served as SCLC headquarters.

To further the efforts to register black voters and to highlight the racism in Alabama, King proposed a Selma-to-Montgomery march to take place on March 7, 1965. With King in Atlanta, Georgia, the procession was led by SNCC volunteers. At the end of the Edmund Pettus Bridge, the marchers were met by dozens of highway patrolmen and city policemen, who attacked the protesters with clubs and other weapons. Amelia Boynton, near the front of the line, was hit by a trooper's club. As she gasped for breath, another trooper struck her on the back of the neck, and she fell unconscious. Hundreds of other marchers were injured. The photographs from the bridge made national television news and sickened hundreds of thousands of Americans, many of whom decided to head to Selma and join forces with the protesters. Other protests were held in eighty cities.

King announced that a new march would be held on March 21. Protected by FBI agents and National Guardsmen, thousands of protesters led by King headed back across Edmund Pettus Bridge and marched toward Montgomery, Alabama. By the time the group successfully reached Montgomery, the number of participants had swelled to over twenty-five thousand.

Amelia Boynton, here, holding up a poster protesting Alabama governor George Wallace, played a critical role in involving the SNCC and the SCLC in Selma civil rights issues.

Mississippi Freedom Democratic Party

Much of the work that Hamer and other activists performed was aimed at increasing black voter registration. A presidential election was held in 1964, and the civil rights organizations wanted black voters to have a voice in choosing the next president. At that time blacks in the state, in fact, were routinely denied their legal right to vote and therefore did not participate in the election process. This prevented them from voting for any candidate, much less the president of the United States.

Presidential candidates then and now are elected through a complicated process that involves such concepts as primaries, caucuses, and conventions. Briefly, caucuses are meetings of select

Fannie Lou Hamer (left) stands outside the 1964 Democratic Convention with the parents of slain civil rights worker Michael Schwerner in protest of the Mississippi Freedom Democratic Party's being denied seats at the convention.

members of a political party, during which the attendees decide which candidate to support; primaries allow voters to pick the candidate. The state then selects delegates to attend the national party convention in order to vote for the candidate that has been selected. The presidential candidate for each party is decided by a majority vote of the delegates; this candidate then picks a vice presidential candidate.

In November the nation votes. The president is determined not by the popular vote, but by the electoral college. Each state is given the number of electors equivalent to that state's number of members in the House of Representatives. A state's electors vote is based on the popular vote in that state; in other words, if the Republican candidate receives the most votes in Tennessee, then Tennessee's eleven electoral votes would go to the Republican candidate. A majority of votes is needed to elect a president.

In 1964 Mississippi's delegation to the Democratic convention was all-white. Black activists in that state did not believe this delegation fairly represented the thousands of blacks who lived in Mississippi. Nor did these delegates support the civil rights movement; some whites were determined to maintain the status quo of white economic and political domination. In fact, the delegates had already decided not to support the Democratic candidate, President Lyndon Johnson, who favored civil rights legislation.

Black activists, including Hamer and others, decided to challenge the all-white delegation. In part to bring attention to the plight of thousands of disenfranchised blacks in the state and the brutality that blacks faced on a daily basis, these activists decided to form a new political party.

In 1964 Hamer was among those who helped found the Mississippi Freedom Democratic Party (MFDP). The members of the MFDP hoped to gain recognition from the national party and replace the white party's delegation to the national convention. They also hoped to play a more active role in the political process and thereby gain fair representation to the Democratic National Convention.

In June 1964 the MFDP organized a committee that established countywide and statewide conventions to select their own delegates to the upcoming Democratic National Convention in Atlantic City, New Jersey. Over eight hundred black delegates attended a state convention held in Jackson, Mississippi, in August 1964. Three women were elected to important delegation positions: Victoria Gray served as national committee woman; Hamer was vice chair of the delegation; and Annie Devine was appointed secretary. Hamer and the other two women were all powerful grassroots organizers. In total sixty-eight delegates were chosen to attend the national convention.

Atlantic City

The MFDP delegation arrived in Atlantic City in late August after traveling there by bus from Mississippi. The group's first order of business was to meet with the convention's credentials committee and present their arguments for being seated as Mississippi's delegation. One by one they told the story of their struggle to win the right to vote. Roy Wilkins of the NAACP testified, as did Martin Luther King Jr. National Public Radio's Lynn Neary explains: "It was a compelling presentation carried live on national television. . . . The most electrifying moment came when Fannie Lou Hamer got up to speak. Hamer, more than anyone, spoke for the sharecroppers and field hands who made up the majority of the Freedom Party."[98]

Hamer's passionate televised appearance before the credential committee brought national attention to the inequities in Mississippi. In this speech Hamer dramatically recounted her experience in Winona, Mississippi, and the beating she had received. Her speech stunned American television viewers. She closed her remarks with an impassioned plea: "If the Freedom Democratic Party is not seated now, I question America—is this America? The land of the free and the home of the brave, where we have to sleep with our telephones off the hook because our lives be threatened daily, because we want to live as decent human beings in America."[99]

Lyndon Johnson, who was running for reelection, was angry that Hamer and her testimony were attracting such attention. Needing southern votes to be reelected and fearing that such testimony could alienate voters, he hastily called the television networks demanding air time to make a speech. Although Johnson was able to preempt much of Hamer's speech, the television news programs all carried film footage of the entire emotional appeal Hamer made. Almost immediately, the Democratic committee was inundated with telephone calls and telegraphs demanding that the MFDP be seated.

Victoria Gray (1926–2006)

Victoria Gray grew up in the tiny village of Palmer's Crossing just outside Hattiesburg, Mississippi. She was reared by her maternal grandparents and attended Wilberforce University in Ohio. She married and traveled to Germany with her husband, who was in the military. While they were later stationed at Fort Meade, Maryland, Gray became a sales representative for a black-owned beauty products firm, called Beauty Queen. After her divorce, Gray returned to Mississippi, where she set up a very successful business selling Beauty Queen products.

Well known in the community, Gray committed herself to the civil rights movement in the early 1960s when young activists from the SNCC came to the area looking to register voters. Gray persuaded her minister to open his church for meetings held by the SNCC. She would later attend a workshop in Dorchester, Georgia, where she met Septima Clark and brought the concept of Citizenship Schools home to Mississippi.

One of the founders of the Mississippi Freedom Democratic Party (MFDP), Gray later ran for office. Civil rights activist and attorney Marian Wright Edelman explains: "As a founding member of the MFDP, she ignored the potential danger to her own safety when she agreed to be the party's candidate to challenge powerful segregationists John Stennis for his Senate seat in 1964." She lost the election but went on to a long career as an educator, campus minister, and grassroots organizer. She died in 2006.

Marian Wright Edelman. "Victoria Gray Adams Was Somebody." *Chicago Defender*, September 6, 2006.

While the MFDP had won the support of the nation, it did not succeed in achieving its goals in a world controlled by powerful politicians. Afraid that southern Democrats might defect to the Republican side, Johnson told his potential vice presidential running mate, Senator Hubert Humphrey, to meet with the MFDP and resolve the conflict or forget about ever being vice president. When Humphrey had finished outlining a compromise, which included the seating of two delegates from the MFDP and a change of rules prior to the 1968 convention, the group turned him down, refusing to accept this token change.

In the meantime, another Democratic politician, Walter Mondale, told the media that the compromise had already been accepted by the MFDP. While this was blatantly untrue, the press had no way of knowing this, so they quickly spread the word that an agreement had been reached. The compromise was then brought to the floor of the full convention, where it was approved. When the news reached the black delegation, Hamer and the others were furious. They did not understand how such a decision could have been made without their approval. They felt betrayed. Historian Michael Cooke summarizes: "Members of the MFDP went to Atlantic City believing that their planned contest of the seats assigned to the state party had a reasonable chance of success. In reality, the MFDP leadership had received an education on how politics at the national level operated."[100]

In the end no one represented Mississippi at the national convention. The all-white delegates walked out, and the black members of the MFDP left in disgust.

Despite the failure to be seated at the convention, the MFDP accomplished a great deal. The party and the inspiring testimony of Hamer helped generate support for the Voting Rights Act, which was passed in 1965. This law outlawed all discriminatory practices such as literacy tests and poll taxes that Mississippi and other southern states used to keep blacks from voting. In addition, after the 1964 convention the Democratic Party resolved that at future conventions no delegation would be seated if anyone in the state was illegally kept from voting. The challenge from Hamer and the MFDP thus eventually brought about an overhaul of the national Democratic Party. The party opened its doors to blacks, women, and minority groups. In 1968 an interracial group from Mississippi was seated at the convention.

Finally, the efforts of the MFDP helped pave the way for the later election of black public officials in the state of Mississippi. By 1994, for instance, the state had over seven hundred black politicians and officials, more than any other state.

Later Work

After the convention, Hamer continued her work for the MFDP. She became one of three people selected to challenge congressional representatives in the election of 1964. The MFDP argued that several congressmen had been elected illegally since black voters had been excluded. Hamer and the MFDP presented fifteen thousand pages of sworn testimony from a variety of sources, documenting the violence that had been directed at potential black voters. This material was presented to the U.S. Congress in an effort to unseat the white congressional representatives from Mississippi. Hamer stated: "The challenge is not simply a challenge to the Congressmen, but a case of deciding between right and wrong. I want to see if the United States Constitution has any meaning for Negroes."[101]

It took eight months before their challenge was heard. On September 17, 1965, Hamer, Annie Devine, and Victoria Gray became the first black women ever seated on the floor of the U.S. House of Representatives. All three women testified before the committee about the inequity of voter registration in Mississippi, but the challenge was dismissed by congressional vote.

The following year, however, the U.S. Fifth Circuit Court of Appeals in *Hamer v. Campbell* nullified the Sunflower County elections that had been upheld by Congress. This was the first time in over one hundred years that a federal court had struck down an election because black voters had been excluded. White candidates, realizing the huge impact black voters could have, began to campaign actively for black votes.

In addition to her MFDP work, Hamer also continued her civil rights activism. She ran but lost a race for a congressional seat in 1964 and a Senate seat in 1971. Hamer lived to see an African American, Robert Clark, elected to the Mississippi legislature in 1968. She was one of the keynote speakers at the 1968 Democratic Convention, receiving a standing ovation. The Mississippi delegation was integrated for the first time in history. She was also part of the delegation at the 1972 convention. Throughout the 1970s Hamer remained active in Mississippi politics and spoke out on civil rights issues, women's rights, and antiwar issues throughout the United States.

Hamer later went back to farmwork and helped establish the Freedom Farm Corporation, a cooperative project that involved black farmers. The corporation was a venture to bring economic self-sufficiency to poor blacks in Mississippi. Seventy homes were built as part of this project. By February 1969 Hamer's organization had received enough money to buy 40 acres (16.2ha) of land, which they leased to the farmers for a minimal fee.

Hamer also worked diligently to provide poor African Americans with food and jobs. Professor Kai Lee elaborates: "For Hamer, a meaningful social movement was one that addressed the everyday needs of people. It made little sense to recruit the disenfranchised to go into a courthouse and register to vote when they

Fannie Lou Hamer was a keynote speaker at the 1968 Democratic National Convention, for which she received a standing ovation.

were worried about eating or having shoes to wear."[102] Throughout her years of civil rights activism, Hamer remained concerned
about poverty; if there was a need for food or clothing, Hamer
found a way to distribute those items.

Hamer died in 1977 after a long struggle with cancer, diabe-
tes, and heart disease. It took two churches to hold all the people
gathered to celebrate her life. Civil rights activist Andrew Young
delivered her eulogy and later wrote: "Mrs. Hamer . . . [became]
one of the most forceful leaders of the Southern movement, her
unique eloquence providing unforgettable testimony to the suffering of black people in the South and the meaning of the struggle to alleviate that suffering."[103] Hamer epitomized the thousands
of black women who fought for equality at the local level. She led
and inspired thousands by her example of hard work as well as
her willingness to die for her beliefs.

Notes

Introduction: Unsung Heroines

1. Lynne Olson. *Freedom's Daughters: The Unsung Heroines of the Civil Rights Movement from 1830 to 1970.* New York: Simon and Schuster, 2001, p. 15.

2. Karen Jackson-Weaver. "An Invisible Calling: The Role of Black Women in the Civil Rights Movement." *African American Pulpit*, October 1, 2006.

3. Quoted in Olson. *Freedom's Daughters*, p. 251.

4. John Lewis with Michael D'Orso. *Walking with the Wind: A Memoir of the Movement.* San Diego: Harcourt, Brace, 1998, p. 214.

5. Quoted in Bettye Collier-Thomas and V.P. Franklin, eds. *Sisters in the Struggle: African American Women in the Civil Rights–Black Power Movement.* New York: New York University Press, 2001, p. 116.

6. Andrew Young. *An Easy Burden: The Civil Rights Movement and the Transformation of America.* New York: Harper Collins, 1996, p. 143.

7. Garry Crystal. "Women and Civil Rights." Civil Rights Movement, August 20, 2010. http://civilrights movement.co.uk/women-civil-rights .html.

Chapter One: Ida B. Wells and the Campaign Against Lynching

8. Jennifer McBride. "Ida B. Wells: Crusade for Justice." Webster University. www.webster.edu/~woolflm/idabwells .html.

9. Quoted in Karenna Gore Schiff. *Lighting the Way: Nine Women Who Changed Modern America.* New York: Hyperion, 2005, p. 2.

10. Schiff. *Lighting the Way*, p. 16.

11. Quoted in McBride. "Ida B. Wells."

12. Clarissa Myrick-Harris. "Against All Odds." *Smithsonian*, July 2002, p. 72.

13. Quoted in Schiff. *Lighting the Way*, p. 19.

14. Quoted in Linda O. McMurry. *To Keep the Waters Troubled: The Life of Ida B. Wells.* New York: Oxford University Press, 1998, p. 139.

15. Quoted in McBride. "Ida B. Wells."

16. Quoted in Sanford Wexler. *The Civil Rights Movement: An Eyewitness History.* New York: Facts On File, 1993, p. 23.

17. Myrick-Harris. "Against All Odds," p. 70.

18. Myrick-Harris. "Against All Odds," p. 74.

19. Schiff. *Lighting the Way*, p. 50.

Chapter Two: Dorothy Height and the National Council of Negro Women

20. Quoted in CBS News. "Dorothy Height, Female Civil Rights Leader Dies." April 29, 2010. www.cbsnews .com/2100-201_162-6413840.html.

21. Quoted in States News Service. "Ecumenical Leaders Recall Dorothy I. Height as a Tireless Supporter of Church Unity." April 20, 2010.

22. Lea E. Williams. "Dorothy Irene Height: A Life Well-Lived." *Phi Kappa Phi Forum*, July 1, 2011, p. 9.

23. Dorothy Height. *Open Wide the Freedom Gates*. New York: Public Affairs, 2003, p. 7.

24. Quoted in Clarence Waldron. "Dr. Dorothy Height: Civil Rights Leader: A Driving Force Behind Social Justice." *Jet*, May 10, 2010, p. 18.

25. Height. *Open Wide the Freedom Gates*, p. 64.

26. Quoted in Height. *Open Wide the Freedom Gates*, p. 115.

27. Quoted in Collier-Thomas and Franklin. *Sisters in the Struggle*, p. 87.

28. Quoted in *PBS NewsHour*. "Open Wide the Freedom Gates." July 17, 2003. www.pbs.org/newshour/bb /race_relations/july-dec03/height _07-18.html.

29. Williams. "Dorothy Irene Height," p. 10.

30. Height. *Open Wide the Freedom Gates*, p. 215.

31. Waldron. "Dr. Dorothy Height," p. 20.

32. Quoted in *PBS NewsHour*. "Open Wide the Freedom Gates."

33. Quoted in Neal Conan. "Dorothy Height: Godmother of Civil Rights." *Talk of the Nation*, NPR, April 20, 2010.

34. Quoted in *Jet*. "Champion of a Righteous Cause." May 17, 2010, pp. 40–41.

35. Quoted in Rosemarie Robotham. "Peaceful Warrior." *Essence*, June 2010, p. 192.

36. Robotham. "Peaceful Warrior," p. 192.

Chapter Three: Septima Clark and the Citizenship Schools

37. Olson. *Freedom's Daughters*, p. 215.

38. Carol Sears Botsch. "Septima Poinsette Clark." University of South Carolina–Aiken, August 30, 2000. www.usca.edu/aasc/clark.htm.

39. Quoted in Collier-Thomas and Franklin. *Sisters in the Struggle*, p. 103.

40. Taylor Branch. *Pillar of Fire: America in the King Years, 1963–1965*. New York: Simon and Schuster, p. 263.

41. Quoted in Vicki L. Crawford, Jacqueline Anne Rouse, and Barbara Woods, eds. *Women in the Civil Rights Movement: Trailblazers and Torchbearers*. Bloomington: Indiana University Press, 1993, p. 92.

42. Taylor Branch. *Parting the Waters: America in the King Years: 1954–1963*. New York: Simon and Schuster, p. 576.

43. Quoted in Katherine Mellen Charron and David P. Cline. "I Train the People to Do Their Own Talking: Septima Clark and Women in the Civil Rights Movement." *Southern Culture*, June 22, 2010.

44. Branch. *Pillar of Fire*, p. 70.

45. Charron and Cline. "I Train the People."

46. Mack T. Hines III and Dianne Reed. "Educating for Social Justice: The Life and Times of Septima Clark in Review." *Advancing Women in Leadership*, January 1, 2007.

47. Olson. *Freedom's Daughters*, p. 223.

48. Quoted in Olson. *Freedom's Daughters*, p. 224.

49. Quoted in Botsch. "Septima Poinsette Clark."

50. Schiff. *Lighting the Way*, p. 258.

Chapter Four: The Women of the Montgomery Bus Boycott

51. Quoted in David Halberstam. *The Fifties*. New York: Fawcett Columbine, 1993, p. 545.

52. Olson. *Freedom's Daughters*, p. 88.

53. Quoted in Donnie Williams with Wayne Greenhaw. *The Thunder of Angels: The Montgomery Bus Boycott and the People Who Broke the Back of Jim Crow*. Chicago: Lawrence Hill, 2006, p. 57.

54. Quoted in Kevin Markey. *One Hundred Most Important Women of the Twentieth Century*. Des Moines, IA: Meredith, 1998, p. 39.

55. Halberstam. *The Fifties*, p. 541.

56. Quoted in Williams. *The Thunder of Angels*, p. 48.

57. Quoted in Herb Boyd. *We Shall Overcome*. Napierville, IL: Sourcebooks, 2004, p. 48.

58. Quoted in Wexler. *The Civil Rights Movement*, p. 70.

59. Denise L. Berkhalter. "Behind the Boycott." *Crisis*, March 1, 2006.

60. Quoted in Henry Hampton and Steve Fayer. *Voices of Freedom: An Oral History of the Civil Rights Movement from the 1950s Through the 1980s*. New York: Bantam, 1990, p. 23.

61. Quoted in Clayborne Carson, ed. *The Autobiography of Martin Luther King, Jr.* New York: Warner, 1998, p. 66.

62. Quoted in Crawford, Rouse, and Woods. *Women in the Civil Rights Movement*, p. 75.

63. Quoted in Wexler. *The Civil Rights Movement*, p. 321.

64. Quoted in Berkhalter. "Behind the Boycott."

Chapter Five: Daisy Bates and School Desegregation

65. Quoted in Juan Williams. "Daisy Bates and the Little Rock Nine." NPR, September 21, 2007. www

.npr.org/templates/story/story.php
?storyId=14563865.

66. Melba Pattillo Beals. *Warriors Don't
Cry: A Searing Memoir of the Battle
to Integrate Little Rock's Central High.*
New York: Washington Square,
1994, p. 33.

67. Linda Reed. "The Legacy of Daisy
Bates." *Arkansas Historical Quarterly*,
April 1, 2000.

68. Quoted in Boyd. *We Shall Overcome*,
p. 57.

69. Quoted in Clayborne Carson, David
J. Garrow, Gerald Gill, Vincent Hard-
ing, and Darlene Clark Hine, eds.
*Eyes on the Prize: Documents, Speeches,
and Firsthand Accounts from the Black
Freedom Struggle, 1954–1960.* New
York: Viking, 1991, p. 98.

70. Halberstam. *The Fifties*, p. 674.

71. Halberstam. *The Fifties*, p. 689.

72. Reed. "The Legacy of Daisy Bates."

73. Quoted in Wexler. *The Civil Rights
Movement*, p. 103.

Chapter Six: Ella Baker, the Spiritual Leader of the Student Nonviolent Coordinating Committee

74. Quoted in Tavis Smiley. "Interview:
Author Barbara Ransby Talks About
the Life and Work of Ella Baker."
NPR, July 15, 2003.

75. Quoted in Olson. *Freedom's Daughters*, p. 235.

76. Quoted in Marilyn Bordwell
DeLaure. "Planting Seeds of Change:

Ella Baker's Radical Rhetoric." *Wom-
en's Studies in Communication*, March
22, 2008.

77. Quoted in DeLaure. "Planting Seeds
of Change."

78. DeLaure. "Planting Seeds of
Change."

79. Collier-Thomas and Franklin. *Sisters
in the Struggle*, p. 10.

80. DeLaure. "Planting Seeds of
Change."

81. Quoted in DeLaure. "Planting Seeds
of Change."

82. Quoted in Crawford, Rouse, and
Woods. *Women in the Civil Rights
Movement*, p. 64.

83. Quoted in Collier-Thomas and Franklin. *Sisters in the Struggle*, p. 188.

84. Quoted in Boyd. *We Shall Overcome*,
p. 100.

85. DeLaure. "Planting Seeds of
Change."

86. Quoted in DeLaure. "Planting Seeds
of Change."

87. Quoted in Crawford, Rouse, and
Woods. *Women in the Civil Rights
Movement*, p. 58.

88. Lewis. *Walking with the Wind*, p. 108.

89. Boyd. *We Shall Overcome*, p. 183.

Chapter Seven: Fannie Lou Hamer and the Mississippi Freedom Democratic Party

90. Quoted in Crawford, Rouse, and
Woods. *Women in the Civil Rights
Movement*, p. 35.

91. Quoted in Collier-Thomas and Franklin. *Sisters in the Struggle*, p. 141.

92. Lewis. *Walking with the Wind*, p. 188.

93. Quoted in Schiff. *Lighting the Way*, p. 286.

94. Quoted in Boyd. *We Shall Overcome*, p. 182.

95. Branch. *Parting the Waters*, p. 819.

96. Olson. *Freedom's Daughters*, p. 262.

97. Quoted in Wexler. *The Civil Rights Movement*, p. 207.

98. Lynn Neary. "Special Report on Mississippi Freedom Democrats—1964."

All Things Considered, NPR, August 27, 1994.

99. Quoted in Neary. "Special Report on Mississippi Freedom Democrats—1964."

100. Michael Cooke. "Mississippi Freedom Democratic Party." *Encyclopedia of African-American Culture and History*, January 1, 2006.

101. Quoted in Collier-Thomas and Franklin. *Sisters in the Struggle*, p. 133.

102. Quoted in Collier-Thomas and Franklin. *Sisters in the Struggle*, p. 154.

103. Young. *An Easy Burden*, p. 152.

For More Information

Books

David A. Adler. *Heroes for Civil Rights*. New York: Holiday House, 2008. This book focuses on many civil rights leaders, including Fannie Lou Hamer and Rosa Parks.

Susan Altman. *Extraordinary African Americans*. New York: Children's, 2001. The author gives brief biographies of many African Americans who contributed to the growth of the United States, including Rosa Parks, Fannie Lou Hamer, and Ella Baker.

Raymond Arsenault. *Freedom Riders: 1961 and the Struggle for Racial Justice*. New York: Oxford University Press, 2006. This book covers the history of the 1961 Freedom Ride, including information on the roles of Ella Baker and Diane Nash.

Molefi Kete Asante. *100 Greatest African Americans*. New York: Prometheus, 2002. This is a biographical encyclopedia with references to a number of women civil rights leaders and figures.

Lisa Frederiksen Bohannon. *Ella Baker and the Civil Rights Movement*. Greensboro, NC: Morgan Reynolds, 2005. A biography of civil rights activist Ella Baker.

Gail Collins. *America's Women: 400 Years of Dolls, Drudges, Helpmates, and Her-oines*. New York: William Morrow, 2003. The author looks at women in the history of America, with a good chapter on the women of the civil rights movement.

Judith Bloom Fradin and Dennis Brindell Fradin. *The Power of One: Daisy Bates and the Little Rock Nine*. New York: Clarion, 2004. The biography of the women who led and supported the nine children who integrated Central High School in Little Rock, Arkansas.

Malu Halasa. *Mary McLeod Bethune*. Philadelphia: Chelsea House, 1989. A biography of civil rights leader Mary McLeod Bethune.

Cheryl Harness. *Rabble Rousers: Twenty Women Who Made a Difference*. New York: Dutton Children's, 2003. Short biographies of several women, including Sojourner Truth, Ida B. Wells-Barnett, and Fannie Lou Hamer.

Toyomi Igus, Veronica Freeman Ellis, Diane Patrick, and Valerie Wilson Wesley. *Great Women in the Struggle*. Orange, NJ: Just Us, 1991. The authors give brief biographies of African American women, many of whom were leaders during the civil rights movement.

Diane McWhorter. *A Dream of Freedom: The Civil Rights Movement from 1954–1968*. New York: Scholastic, 2004.

An overall look at some of the key moments of the civil rights movement.

Charlotte S. Waisman and Jill S. Tietjen. *Her Story: A Timeline of the Women Who Changed America*. New York: Collins, 2008. This book presents brief biographies of numerous women who helped change life in America.

Periodicals

Denise Watson Batts. "Barbara Johns: Quiet Teen Made a Loud Statement Against Injustice." *Virginian-Pilot* (Norfolk, VA), February 10, 2008.

Staci Bush. "History of Black Women's Organizations." *Sacramento Observer*, January 26, 1994.

Fort Lauderdale (FL) Westside Gazette. "Fannie Lou Hamer—1917–1977; 'I'm Sick and Tired of Being Sick and Tired.'" March 24, 2004.

Journal of Blacks in Higher Education. "Daisy Lee Gatson Bates, 1914–1999." January 31, 2000.

John A. Kirk. "Crisis at Central High." *History Today*, September 2007.

Anthony R. Kugler. "Legendary Leaders." *Cobblestone*, April 1, 2008.

Dee Dee Risher. "To Be a Light Bearer." *Other Side*, January 1, 1998.

Sarah Thuesen. "Learning from the Long Civil Rights Movement's First Generation: Virginia Foster Durr." *Southern Culture*, June 22, 2010.

Internet Sources

Gender in Civil Rights Movement. "Jo Ann Robinson and the Women's Political Council." www.shmoop.com/civil-rights-desegregation/gender.html.

Barbara Harris. "Ella Baker: Backbone of the Civil Rights Movement." Jackson Advocate News Service, March 26–April 1, 2009. www.jacksonadvocateonline.com/?p=2877.

Howard University Library System. "Fannie Lou Hamer: Woman of Courage." www.howard.edu/library/Reference/Guides/Hamer/default.htm.

Tavis Smiley. "Civil Rights Activist Diane Nash." PBS, May 10, 2011. www.pbs.org/wnet/tavissmiley/interviews/civil-rights-activist-diane-nash.

Website

Ella Baker Biography, AmericansWho Tell the Truth (http://americanswhotellthetruth.org/pgs/portraits/Ella_Baker.php). A website that offers a brief biography of Ella Baker.

Index

Picture Credits

Cover: © Seqoya/Shutterstock.com;
   © Everett Collection, Inc./Alamy

© AFP/Getty Images, 77

© AP Images, 9

© AP Images/Gene Smith, 48

© AP Images/Haraz N. Ghanbari, 38

© AP Images/Harold Valentine, 64

© AP Images/Jack Harris, 91

© AP Images/Montgomery County
   Sheriff's office, 57

© AP Images/Richard Drew, 59

© Bettmann/Corbis, 33, 68, 70, 88, 106

© Bob Adelman/Corbis, 47

© Corbis, 87

© Everett Collection Inc./Alamy, 13, 14,
   24, 29, 62, 82, 96

© Express Newspapers/Getty Images,
   27

© Express Newspapers/L360/Getty
   Images, 10

© Fotosearch/Getty Images, 23

© Francis Miller/Time & Life Pictures /
   Getty Images, 99

© George Karger/Pix Inc./Time Life
   Pictures/Getty Images, 30

© Grey Villet/Time & Life Pictures/Getty
   Images, 54

© Karen Kasmauski/Corbis, 42

© Leemage/UIG via Getty Images, 17

© Marie Hansen/Time & Life Pictures/
   Getty Images, 85

© Robert Abbott Sengstacke/Getty
   Images, 100

© Thomas D. McAvoy/Time & Life
   Pictures/Getty Images, 73, 78

© Tony Pescatore/NY Daily News Archive
   via Getty Images, 34

© Weinstein Company/Courtesy Everett
   Collection, 45

© World History Archive/Alamy, 20

© ZUMA Wire Service/Alamy, 51

About the Author

Anne Wallace Sharp is the author of the adult book *Gifts*; several children's books, including *Daring Pirate Women*; and twenty other titles for Lucent Books. She has also written numerous magazine articles for both adults and juveniles. A retired registered nurse, Sharp has a degree in history. Her interests include reading, travel, and spending time with her grandchildren, Jacob and Nicole. She lives in Beavercreek, Ohio.